The New Spiritual Exercises

In the Spirit of Pierre Teilhard de Chardin

LOUIS M. SAVARY

Paulist Press
New York / Mahwah, NJ

Cover design by Joy Taylor
Book design by Lynn Else

Quotations from *The Spiritual Exercises of St. Ignatius* by George Ganss, SJ, are used with permission: © The Institute of Jesuit Sources, St. Louis, MO. All rights reserved.

Library of Congress Cataloging-in-Publication Data

Savary, Louis M.
    The new spiritual exercises: in the spirit of Pierre Teilhard de Chardin / Louis M. Savary.
        p. cm.
    ISBN 978-0-8091-4695-6 (alk. paper)
    1. Spiritual life—Catholic Church. 2. Spiritual exercises. 3. Ignatius, of Loyola, Saint, 1491–1556. Exercitia spiritualia. 4. Teilhard de Chardin, Pierre. I. Title.
    BX2178.S28 2010
    248.3—dc22

                                                                                    2010023722

Published by Paulist Press
997 Macarthur Boulevard
Mahwah, New Jersey 07430

www.paulistpress.com

Printed and bound in the
United States of America

Contents

Contents

For Patricia H. Berne, my wife, partner,
friend, inspiration, and guide.

Acknowledgments

My biggest thanks go to four Jesuit classmates from my Jesuit years, all experts in giving the Spiritual Exercises but coming from quite different perspectives: George Aschenbrenner, SJ, Roger Haight, SJ, Matthew Linn, SJ, and Brian McDermott, SJ. I shared with them much of the text, piece by piece, and they gave very helpful comments, keeping me focused on my task. Like them, I made the original Ignatian Exercises under many Jesuit retreat directors, starting with my novice master Thomas Gavigan, SJ.

Additional contemporary Jesuits, Ignatian scholars whose writings I used as research, include David Coghlan, SJ, Robert Faricy, SJ, David Fleming, SJ, George Ganss, SJ, W. Henry Kenney, SJ, Thomas King, SJ, George Lane, SJ, Christopher Mooney, SJ, John O'Malley, SJ, Juan Luis Segundo, SJ, James Skehan, SJ, and Joseph Tetlow, SJ.

In addition to Teilhard in his own writings, there are the many Jesuits who, over the years, influenced my understanding of Teilhard, most especially my cosmology professor Robert Johann, SJ. I read the books of those who knew Teilhard personally and first introduced us to his life and thought, such as Pierre Leroy, SJ, Claude Tresmontant, SJ, and Henri de Lubac, SJ.

I thank the people of the American Teilhard Society who supported my work, especially John Grim, Mary Evelyn Tucker, Arthur Fabel, and Kathleen Duffy, SSJ. I am grateful to the late Father Lawrence Boadt, CSP, Paul McMahon, and others on the team at Paulist Press who believed in my dream and helped make my manuscript worthy of publishing.

In addition, there are many who, over the past half century, have encouraged, supported, and enriched my Teilhardian workshops and writings, including: Father Thomas Composto, Dan and Rose Lucey, Father Gerard Fahey, Robert Fritz, Sister Sadie Nesser, RC, Sister Olga Neft, OSF, Father Charles Topper, Sister Marylouise Fennell, RSM, Edward Zogby, SJ, Len Sroka, Thomas Francis, OSCO, Judy

Cannato, Richard Rohr, OSF, Clare Crawford-Mason, Bob Mason, and Sister Mary Madden, SSJ.

Thanks to enthusiastic supporters from Tampa: Father Austin Mullen, Father Len Piotrowski, Father Joseph Musco, and Father Jose Colina; Deacons John Alvarez and Gregory Kovalesky; Peter and Mary Esseff, Florence Murphy, Thomas Kochansky, Julie Cate, Sister Cathy Cahill, OSF, and the team at the Franciscan Center.

Finally, thanks to supporters from Orleans, MA, including Father Bob Powell, Ed Daly, Judy Burt-Walker, and others. I consider this book a work in progress.

Introduction

For four centuries, *The Spiritual Exercises of Saint Ignatius Loyola* have been a powerful and resilient force in shaping Christian life and spirituality. *The Exercises*, as they are familiarly called in the Society of Jesus, have inspired and energized many thousands of Jesuits and others. Just as well-designed physical exercises can help improve and renew one's physical life, Ignatius believed that well-designed spiritual exercises can help improve and renew one's spiritual life.

This book presents a spiritual renewal system for contemporary believers based on Ignatius' *Spiritual Exercises* and inspired by the modern insights of Jesuit priest-scientist Pierre Teilhard de Chardin (1881–1955)—a reenvisioning of the original *Exercises* as *Teilhard might envision and re-create them if he were alive today*. While Teilhard never actually wrote such a book, these new Exercises are my vision of how a twenty-first century Teilhard might have adapted Ignatius' classic work.

In the Teilhardian spirit, these *New Spiritual Exercises* do not focus primarily on personal sin and saving one's soul, but upon the graces and blessings God gives us for consciously creating a positive difference in our world. They are based on the scriptural revelation that God has a great project going on—much more than just keeping souls from falling into sin and hell—and that we are all invited to become fully and actively involved in this divine project. Saint Paul clearly recognized and promoted this project (see Eph 3 and 4). It is a cosmic project God envisioned almost fourteen billion years ago at the first moment of creation. That great creation project is still going forward, and with humanity's creative help it will gain momentum. In *The New Spiritual Exercises* you are invited to become a co-creator with God of the divine vision, formulated by Jesus, "That all may be one as you, Father, are in me and I am in you" (John 17:21).

Teilhard the Prophet

Teilhard was Ignatian to his core, and he remained faithfully committed to the Society of Jesus until the day he died, despite decades of rejection by his own religious superiors and other influential people in the church.

In a prophetic spirit, Teilhard was presenting, as early as the 1920s, evolutionary theological ideas in his talks, essays, and correspondence—ideas about integrating Christianity and evolution, revelations about the nature of God flowing from modern scientific discoveries, the central importance of the universal Body of Christ in everyday spirituality, the emerging "noosphere" (the collective mind and heart of humanity) as the tip of an evolutionary arrow, and the innate longing of all creation, not just humanity, to reach the fulfillment the Creator has always desired for it. In those earlier days, most minds in the church were not ready to hear Teilhard's radically fresh insights, let alone grasp them, digest them, and integrate them into their theological and spiritual mind-set. Today, I think we are ready.

Teilhard and the Ignatian Exercises

Teilhard faithfully made the Ignatian Exercises during his annual retreat each year. However, in his retreat notes he hinted at a growing need for their "transposition," which is an interesting concept.

For example, in music, to transpose means to shift into a new key. In its new key, the song is not changed but acquires a fresh expression and makes a more powerful impression. In the new key, different orchestral instruments often carry the melody and give it a new feeling and flavor. Teilhard is suggesting that there is the need to write Ignatian spirituality in a new key and let the instruments of science and evolution express the melody of God's kingdom in a way we have not heard before. In his two books, *The Phenomenon of Man* and *The Divine Milieu*, Teilhard presents the core of what might be his way of approaching this transposition.

Ignatius' Exercises as Evolutionary

Without doubt, four centuries ago the traditional *Spiritual Exercises* of Ignatius Loyola (1491–1556) were themselves an evolutionary document for their time. For example, Ignatius introduced new structured methods of prayer, well-ordered steps for meditation and contemplation, a systematized set of rules for spiritual directors guiding retreatants, methods of discernment, the daily examination of conscience, a method for journaling insights from prayer, frequent reception of Holy Communion, and many other things. Few would challenge the claim that Ignatius' *Exercises* were themselves an evolutionary force in the sixteenth century.

However, from a twenty-first-century perspective, the *Exercises* as written do not—and, in fact, cannot—truly encompass the broader needs of today's spiritual seekers involved in a highly interwoven global situation with its complex and rapidly changing scientific, ecological, economic, diplomatic, political, ethical, and interfaith concerns.

Although, for years, Ignatian spiritual directors have been adapting and updating the traditional *Exercises* in various ways, *no one has yet attempted to provide an integrated spiritual system for believers of today as simple, direct, and comprehensive as Ignatius' Spiritual Exercises.*

Similarities and Differences

The New Spiritual Exercises will follow, for the most part, the same structure and order of the original four weeks of the *Spiritual Exercises of Saint Ignatius*. People who have already made the traditional Exercises will recognize its key elements here, such as the four-week structure; the Annotations, Principle and Foundation, and Examen; meditations on the Kingdom, the Two Standards, the Three Classes of Men, the Three Degrees of Humility; Discernment of Spirits; the *Contemplatio*, etc. However, those who are new to the Exercises can easily follow the flow of the process in these pages.

The New Spiritual Exercises will be unlike the original *Spiritual Exercises* in at least three ways, inspired by Teilhard.

First, for Teilhard, because the creation of the universe is a primary act of God's self-expression and an important part of God's self-revelation to us, *creation's evolving story must be integrated into any contemporary spirituality.* Even the ancient psalmist was aware that all of nature was trying to tell us about God and God's love for us (see Psalm 19:1–4). In our day, science is increasing our ability to "read" creation's story.

Second, for Teilhard, *to love God requires loving the world as well,* since what God brought forth in the evolving cosmos is precisely God's loving self-expression. For Teilhard, because God loves the totality of creation unconditionally and wants it to evolve to its destined completion, we too should learn to love the cosmos with a passion. Our challenge in spirituality is to realize how totally integrated we humans are with all creation and how best to work toward creation's divinely desired evolutionary fulfillment.

Third, for Teilhard, this new evolutionary scientific information (less than a century old) allows us *to look at all of creation in its multibillion-year history and give a richer and more concrete meaning to what God is trying to do in the world.* Saint Paul described God's "hidden purpose" (Eph 3:9–10) as "building the Body of Christ" (Eph 4:1–6, 13). Jesus expressed it in his prayer "That all may be one as you, Father, are in me and I am in you" (John 17:21). The church's tradition tries to express this oneness that God is trying to accomplish as "building the Mystical Body of Christ." Teilhard's vision of what God is trying to do is what I like to call the "Christ Project."

The Christ Project

God's Christ Project encompasses the entire evolving universe, and its aim is to bring creation (along with all of us) back to God, fully conscious of our divine origin and divine destiny. This "bringing it all back to God" is what Ignatius, four centuries ago, could only glimpse as the purpose of the call of Christ in his Kingdom meditation.

One main reason for creating *The New Spiritual Exercises* is to provide a clearer way for today's loving and generous people to grasp this divine plan, this Christ Project—building the Body of Christ, the Cosmic Christ—and to commit themselves to it.

Like many Christians throughout the centuries, Saint Teresa of Avila, who died in 1582, grasped the magnificence of the Christ

Body that lives today. She wrote the following lyrical passage, which still stirs the heart of everyone who reads it.

> Christ has no body now but yours,
> no hands, no feet on Earth but yours.
> Yours are the only eyes
> with which his compassion
> can still look out on a troubled world.
> Yours are the only feet
> with which he can go about doing good.
> Yours are the only hands
> with which he can bring his blessing to his people.
> Christ has no body now on Earth but yours.

Magnificent and compassionate as this vision of Teresa's is, it does not provide a vision of the grand work God has planned for this Christ Body on Earth. It pictures God's work rather generally, as "doing good" and bringing "blessings." A clearer and more comprehensive picture of the Christ Project would begin to emerge with Teilhard's insights. For him, the Christ Project becomes apparent in our time as a new revelation flowing from the integration of theology with recent scientific discoveries.

In the text, the terms *Christ Project* and the universal *Body of Christ* are used interchangeably. The term *Christ Project* emphasizes the universality of God's evolutionary plan inviting all humanity to be conscious of it and involved in it, while the Body of Christ image, as in Teresa's words, reminds us that this project is very personal and interpersonal, the work of an immense community, a communion of saints.

Understanding the Christ Project and the need for the involvement of everyone, not just Christians, is central to these new spiritual exercises. When this is understood, planetary ecological issues such as global warming, overpopulation, and saving the planet become the responsibility of the universal Body of Christ; planetary political issues such as international law, worldwide poverty, emerging diseases, the proliferation of nuclear weapons, and terrorism become issues under the responsibility of the universal Body of Christ; planetary psychological challenges such as the need to develop a cosmic consciousness, a new systems-thinking mind-set, and an attitude that pursues continual improvement in all areas of human and eco-logical development become the responsibility of the Christ Body. No contemporary formulation of spirituality can ignore these responsibilities of the Christ Body and the universal call to support the grand project that God assigned to his son.

Saint Paul referred to this Christ Project as "the mystery [of the Body of Christ] that was kept secret for long ages but is now disclosed, and through the prophetic writings is made known to all the Gentiles, according to the command of the eternal God" (Rom 16:25–26). God will see that this project is accomplished (Isa 55:10–11).

The culmination and completion of the Christ Project is what Teilhard called the Omega Point. In this sense, the Christ Project might also be called the Omega Project.

A Change in Focus

This book is focused much more on people wanting God's work on Earth to succeed and freely choosing to give themselves to that work, rather than being primarily concerned about their indi-vidual salvation—getting into heaven. For Teilhard, it is God's Christ Project work on Earth that must be of primary importance to those who want to be co-workers with Christ. For many, this will require putting on a new mind-set, a new way of thinking about oneself in relation to others. In this new mind-set, people will no longer view themselves simply as independent persons seeking individual salva-tion, but will rather see themselves as interdependent parts of a greater whole, all of us working side-by-side on the Christ Project.

For Teilhard, although each individual soul is intimately known and unconditionally loved by God, in the end the one Person that God wants to "save" and bring to perfection is the cosmic-sized Christ, in whom lives the entire universe that God lovingly created and set into an evolutionary process almost fourteen billion years ago (Eph 1:9–10).

Some people have asked me how they might explain to others the Christ Project in simple, nonreligious terms and show how every-one can be a part of it. The Christ Project might be summarized in two statements: (1) *We humans are not separate from this planet nor from anyone or anything else on it or in it;* and (2) *we need to uplift everyone and everything on it or in it.* The verb *uplift* is to be taken in its broadest context. We need to uplift everyone, individually and collectively—from poverty, from hunger, from ignorance, from servitude of one form or another, from lack of purpose and meaning, and so on.

In a Teilhardian approach to the Exercises, Ignatius' theme of *magis* ("giving greater service to God") takes an expanded and evolutionary meaning. Working "for the greater glory of God" means more than simply working harder, faster, longer, more efficiently, etc., but rather working more lovingly, more gratefully, more consciously, and more focused on promoting the development of the universal Body of Christ.

In the Teilhardian perspective, another key shift in thought is to recognize the ever-increasing growth in the size and complexity of human society. Christ-workers today need to be found not only among clergy and consecrated religious people, but among scientists, physicians, psychologists, other healthcare personnel, pharmacists, teachers, fitness trainers, mathematicians, physicists, biologists, chemists, geneticists, engineers, architects, bankers, financial experts, investors, industrialists, computer people, information experts, people in the transportation industry, people in the service professions, marketers, politicians, inventors, entrepreneurs, diplomats, journalists, novelists, film producers, media people, and all others who can in some way continue to push the evolutionary envelope. The Christ Project needs front-line workers as well as leaders. It needs the poor as well as the rich. It needs everyone who can make a positive difference, no matter how small.

Furthermore, today's Christ-workers need to be team players, community builders, peacemakers, and researchers; creative, flexible, resilient, energetic, forgiving, innovative, optimistic people. They need to learn to pray together, to contemplate together, and to envision and create a new future together. Suggestions for small teams to make the New Spiritual Exercises together and to enter into contemplation together are offered in the text.

Today's Christ-workers can never be satisfied with the status quo, but are rather intent on maximizing potentials and stretching the horizon, envisioning what does not yet exist and making it happen. This is what Teilhard called "loving the not-yet."

In the Christ Project there is no room for apathy.

A Project of Love

The New Spiritual Exercises is all about love—God's love and human love—how to give it and how to respond to it. To enter into these exercises is to plunge into the experience of divine love and human love in a way you may not have thought about before.

So, whenever you find the text becoming too intellectual, stop for a moment and remind yourself that the Exercises are primarily about love given and received. Think about all the people in your life who love you and have loved you. If you need more time to get back in the proper mood, think too of all the people, animals, and places you have loved.

I sometimes think that animals, especially pets, were put into our lives to teach us how to freely give and receive love and affection, and to teach us how unconditionally God loves us.

A Personal Calling

Sharing Teilhard's spirituality with contemporary people has always been a clear personal inner drive for me. I was captivated by his ideas from my first encounter with them some years ago. In that moment I recognized the radical truth, validity, and newness of Teilhard's ideas, and I also felt called to spend the remaining years of my life spreading his ideas. I felt a calling, too, to make his ideas a bit easier for people to understand than in his original texts.

Ignatius always taught his fellow Jesuits that, when presented with ideas or behaviors that are strange, unusual, questionable, or appear to be wrong, they should always begin by trying to find what might be good, useful, or inspiring in that person's ideas, rather than to criticize them or condemn them outright. Jesuits call this approach giving someone a "plus sign," that is, to look first for the positive in what is being offered and to assume that the person offering it wants the best and is operating with good intentions. Therefore, I am asking those who read this book to please give me a "plus sign," for I truly want the best and my intentions are good.

I welcome any suggestions for improvement, since this is really my first attempt at a systematic "transposition" of the Exercises. I need to know if the new Exercises work, how they work, and who finds them helpful. After all, Ignatius did his first drafts of the *Spiritual Exercises* as early as 1521, when he was about thirty years old, and he continued to revise and adapt them for the next twenty-seven years. Even after they were formally published in 1548, Ignatius continued to improve them.

In Ignatius' own text, I noticed that he too asked the readers of his Exercises to give him a "plus sign." Before the First Exercise and after the Annotations, Ignatius places this statement on its own page. I suspect Ignatius saw himself as the "neighbor" he refers to.

Presupposition
That both the giver and the receiver of the Spiritual Exercises may be of greater help and benefit to each other, it should be proposed that every good Christian ought to be more eager to put a good interpretation on a neighbor's statement than to condemn it. Further, if one cannot interpret it favorably, one should ask how the other means it. If that meaning is wrong, one should correct the person with love. And if this is not enough, one should search out every appropriate means through which, by understanding the statement in a good way, it may be saved. (22)[1]

As you read these pages, I ask you to see me too as the "neighbor."

Louis M. Savary
July 31, 2010
Feast Day of St. Ignatius Loyola

1. The number in parentheses after any quotation from *The Spiritual Exercises of St. Ignatius* refers to a specific paragraph in his text. Jesuits use this numbering system for consistency, to coordinate and compare various translations of the original Spanish and Latin texts. Throughout this book, with permission, I have used the 1992 translation of the *Exercises* made by George E. Ganss, SJ, published by the Institute of Jesuit Sources in St. Louis, Missouri.

Your Purpose and Intention

The New Spiritual Exercises presents a spirituality of action. It involves your free will and your choices. It assumes you come to this powerful process with a specific intention or purpose—that you have come asking, searching, or knocking for something (Matt 7:7). *If you are knocking on God's door, it helps if you know what you want from God.*

Perhaps you have come to change the nature of your work or ministry. Perhaps you are in transition from one job to another. Perhaps you are struggling with an important relationship change. Perhaps you want to reinvigorate your work or your prayer. Perhaps you are in a crisis of faith. Perhaps recently you have lost a friend or some opportunity has been closed to you. Perhaps you face living with a serious illness. Perhaps you feel old and useless. Perhaps you feel full of energy and have no idea how best to direct it.

If you are making these Spiritual Exercises under a director or guide, he or she will usually ask you about your purpose during your first meeting. If you are making them without a guide, you should explore your purpose.

A Moment of Prayer

Take a moment to savor the question: *Why have I come?* Ask yourself, "Is it doubt or confusion that brought me to this time and place? Is it some positive inner movement wanting to find expression? What do I hope to find?" Let yourself love and appreciate the question(s) you bring with you.

In your journal write out now, as best you can, what your purpose is in wanting to make the Exercises at this time. Make a note of your feelings and emotions as well.

Then, once your purpose is formulated, take some time to imagine yourself knocking on God's door, and when you feel God's presence (as in sensing the opening of a door), express your purpose

1

to God, asking that you succeed in accomplishing the reason for which you have come. Whatever it is, let God know what you are experiencing and what you seek.

Eucharist and *The New Spiritual Exercises*

Ignatius understood that the meaning and purpose of the Exercises is summed up in the Eucharist. The Eucharist is the daily living reminder that everything in creation is evolving and that the work of the Christ Project continues.

For Teilhard, the Christ that comes upon the altar at Mass is, of course, the Christ of all time, yesterday, today, and forever. But, for Teilhard, on the altar today it is important to recognize the Christ who lives today, with his evolving universal Body that holds in existence each of us and all of creation. On the altar is he in whom, at this moment, we all live and move and have our being.

It may feel impossible to imagine the Lord of the Universe contained in a piece of bread or a drop of wine, but that is what we are called in faith to do. Teilhard's dream was to teach people to "see" with spiritual eyes the magnificent cosmic Christ Body in the appearance of bread and wine.

The Eucharist represents an eternally new Christ come alive for us each day at Mass. Each day over the Earth, people are bringing to the building of the Body of Christ new acts of kindness, compassion, forgiveness, peace, friendship, discovery, and consciousness. Each day, worldwide, in millions of places individuals and groups are caring for the Earth, bringing people closer together, seeking peace and understanding, cooperating in projects that will help make the world a better place. All these contributions add to, enhance, and renew the evolving Body of Christ that was on the altar yesterday. Tomorrow, and each next day, members of the Body of Christ will add new elements, more unity, more love, more cohesion, and more consciousness—something that is "not yet." In this way, the Body of Christ continues to evolve along its divinely destined trajectory toward the fullness God has envisioned for it. This is the work of the Christ Project.

The Eucharist gives special nourishment and life to this grand project.

Keeping a Journal

Keeping a journal during this spiritual process is as important as having a copy of *The New Spiritual Exercises* to follow.

During this soul-opening process, you will experience many graces and insights. You may make connections between your life experiences and your new insights. Given the complexity of this process, it is sometimes easy to forget the gifts and graces received. Therefore, keep journaling this process as it is happening. Keep a record of the gifts and graces of what is going on inside you, including your resistance as well as your eagerness, your discouragement and your enthusiasm, the issues with which you are struggling and those about which you feel confident and clear. Both kinds of experiences—darkness as well as light—are filled with God's grace and love. God is with you in all of them. This is the valuable work of journaling.

Saint Ignatius was a faithful and almost compulsive journal-keeper. Starting from the first days of his spiritual conversion and continuing throughout his life, he filled many copybooks or spiritual diaries with notes of his spiritual journey and experiences. He often reviewed these pages and shared his insights with others. Ignatius encouraged all his Jesuits to keep daily records of their spiritual development, especially to keep a written review of the wisdom gained each day during prayer.

Teilhard, too, was an avid journal-keeper. During his three decades in quasi-exile in China, he said that he spent half an hour each morning after breakfast keeping a journal of his experiences and insights.

Suggested Activity

As you begin these spiritual exercises, enter on the first page of your journal your name, date, and place. If it is a directed retreat, you

3

may note your director's name. If it is a group retreat, enter the names of others you know who may have entered into this spiritual process with you.

Use your journal to keep a record of your experiences throughout the entire process of your retreat. Use it after each prayer experience and even *during* some prayer experiences. Use it to record and reflect upon other suggested spiritual practices as well as sacramental and liturgical events. Use it to record what goes on during conferences with your guide or director. And use it to record any insights or awareness that may occur at any other times.

Reflection after Each Prayer

Wisely, Ignatius instructed all retreatants that a written reflection after each prayer experience was essential. Even if you are rushed, he told his Jesuits, close your formal prayer early enough to save time for doing a written reflection. He insisted that the written reflection was an integral part of any prayer. Your journal entries are a record of your encounters with God. They deserve to be recorded and not to be forgotten.

Journal during Prayer

A number of the meditations and contemplations in the New Spiritual Exercises call for you to write things or to compile lists *as you pray*. Do this by writing in your journal during the prayer time. After the prayer period, be sure to spend time with your journal, summarizing your reflections. Always give date and time of an entry as well as a title of the event being journaled.

Weekly Review

You may also spend at least an hour profitably at the end of each Week of the Exercises to review your journal and list the graces and insights you have received during that Week.

Annotations

Ignatius presented a series of twenty Annotations at the beginning of the *Spiritual Exercises* to establish certain instructions both for retreatants making the Exercises and to those guiding and giving them. These Annotations remain excellent suggestions for people seeking spiritual growth today. Here are the twenty Annotations of Ignatius slightly adapted for use here—plus a number of new ones. You will notice that some are for the retreatant, while many are suggestions for the spiritual guide.

1. A System for Spiritual Development

People today use well-designed workout routines to strengthen and improve their bodies and achieve a kind of physical freedom. In a similar way, there are well-designed Spiritual Exercises to maintain and strengthen your spiritual life in order to achieve a kind of spiritual clarity and freedom. For Ignatius, such inner freedom was reached when you were able to let go of all inner disorder and misguided attachments and thus were able to seek and find what God wanted you to do or accomplish with your life. This book, a system for spiritual development, is designed especially for Christians, but may be adapted for those of other faiths.

Note: During the days when you are doing these Spiritual Exercises, it is important that you eat healthily and do physical exercise daily. Discuss with your spiritual guide the time you plan to spend in physical activity and any change in eating habits you plan to make.

2. Soul Satisfaction

The person guiding others in this process should introduce the retreatant(s) to each exercise simply and without great explanation. Introductions are also often provided in the text. It is best when the person doing an exercise comes to realize a truth or has an insight.

In this way, they will gain more spiritual benefit and soul-satisfaction than if the guide provides the insights.

3. The Colloquy

Typically, each prayer time usually begins with the retreatant using the intellect and imagination, and is concluded with what Ignatius calls a "colloquy" (a personal prayerful encounter with the Creator, Christ, the Holy Spirit, Mary, or one or other of the saints). When addressing the holy ones, Ignatius advises, "greater reverence is demanded of us than when we are using the intellect to understand" (3).

4. Four Weeks

The Spiritual Exercises are divided into four "Weeks" with each Week having its own specific aim or purpose. In order for the retreatant to achieve each Week's special purpose, a Week may need to be less or more than seven days. In general, the Four Weeks in their fullest expression usually take about thirty days.

5. Courage and Generosity

Retreatants are asked to enter into the Exercises with great courage and generosity, freely inviting God to make total use of their person and abilities.

6. Movements of the Spirit

If the guide notices that a retreatant seems to have no "spiritual movements," such as experiencing consolation or desolation, inner peace or disturbance, the guide should inquire whether the retreatant is faithfully doing the Spiritual Exercises, keeping a journal, and observing these suggestions.

7. The Guide's Gentleness

If the guide sees a particular retreatant is discouraged or finding the process upsetting, difficult, or burdensome, the guide should treat this person very gently and indulgently. The guide should not be hard on or show dissatisfaction with this person, but help get him or her ready for future consolation and inner peace.

8. The Guide as Teacher

If the guide sees that a retreatant needs instruction on recognizing the different movements of the human spirit, the guide can explain these spiritual dynamics as needed.

9. Know Your Retreatant

If a retreatant is not well acquainted with spiritual matters, is grossly self-focused, and is easily tempted away from service to God, the guide should not explain the more subtle spiritual dynamics of temptation, since they may be more confusing and harmful to such a retreatant. Besides, such suggestions will make little or no sense to that person.

10. Spiritual Dynamics

However, when a retreatant is being tempted early on—as Ignatius says, "under the appearance of good"—the guide may introduce the more subtle spiritual dynamics.

11. Stay Focused

The guide should encourage retreatants to stay focused on the aim and purpose of the Week they are in, and not try to figure out what is going to happen in or what the aim of a future Week may be. During each meeting with a retreatant, it is wise for the guide to remind the retreatant of the general aim and purpose of that Week.

12. Temptation to Slack Off

As a retreatant, you are expected to give the full time to each exercise, and not cut it short, which people are often tempted to do. You should feel content that you have given the full time—rather more than less—to the exercise.

13. Agere Contra

When you are feeling consolation and fervor during a spiritual exercise, it is easier to remain in it for the full time than when you are feeling tired, bored, or discouraged. Ignatius suggests that in times of boredom, discouragement, or desolation, in order to act against the inner discomfort and resistance, you should stay with the exercise a little longer than the required time. Ignatius called this extra push *agere contra*, meaning, "to move in a different direction." For example, when a sailboat is sailing into a heavy headwind, the sailor knows it is useless to continue going directly into the wind, so he begins tacking. He goes in another direction.

Note: When inner discomfort arises during prayer, it is important to understand that Ignatius is not asking you to grit your teeth and force yourself to keep at it, as a kind of self-punishment for your inner discomfort or resistance. To do that is to fight against yourself, to make yourself your own enemy, to bring shame and guilt upon yourself for the very real feelings of boredom or discouragement you are experiencing. Rather, focus your attention precisely on those negative feelings—boredom, resistance, and the like—and see those feelings, not as something to be rejected and despised, but as being surrounded by God's love. Bring this shadowy side of yourself to God to be held and healed by God in safety and love. God rejects no part of you. If God loved only the pure and good side of you, God would love only half of you—and maybe not the best half! The totality of you is what lives and moves and has being in God.

14. No Quick Decisions

As a retreatant, be careful not to make any rash decisions, promises, or vows during the process, especially when you feel much consolation and fervor in your prayer. Thank God for the consolation since it is a special gift. Discuss such "inner movements" with your guide. And hold off on making quick decisions.

15. Don't Influence

A guide should be very careful not to influence a major decision of a retreatant either one way or the other, but as Ignatius says, "while standing by like the pointer of a scale in equilibrium, to allow the Creator to deal immediately with the creature and the creature with its Creator and Lord" (15).

16. Watch Motivation

Suppose a retreatant is facing a major life decision between two or more opportunities. And suppose that person comes to the Spiritual Exercises favoring one opportunity over the others, "not for the honor and glory of God our Lord or for the spiritual welfare of souls, but primarily for one's own temporal advantages and interests" (16). In such a case, invite the retreatant to pray that his or her motive for making a major choice be primarily the service of God.

17. Be a Guide, Not a Confessor

The guide should not inquire about the retreatant's personal life or confessional material, but help the retreatant achieve the purpose for which he or she has come to the Exercises. It is more important that the guide focus on the various "inner movements" happening in the person day by day. By knowing these movements, the guide can suggest spiritual exercises appropriate to the person's needs. It is also useful for a guide to remember each retreatant's purpose for making the Exercises as well as to keep a daily record of that person's spiritual process and progress.

18. A Judgment Call

For such persons who are unable to enter the Spiritual Exercises with the requisite spiritual maturity and generosity, some of the easier exercises, such as the Examen and other meditations of the First Week, may be suggested. Such people may also be encouraged to seek the Sacrament of Reconciliation and to receive the Eucharist more frequently.

19. Adapting the Exercises

Those who wish to make the Spiritual Exercises in their entirety but are unable to set aside thirty days for it may come for direction to a guide once or twice a week, who will adapt the Exercises in a way most beneficial to such persons.

20. A Secluded Place

Those who desire to get the most from the Exercises should select a quiet place separate from all ordinary concerns, where in privacy they may attend Mass each day and perform the Exercises without fear of being distracted by the daily matters of family, work, etc.

Some Additional Annotations

21. Journal Keeping

Each retreatant should keep a detailed handwritten journal of his or her *Exercises* experiences, from beginning to end. Note the date and time of day for each entry. See suggestions in the section Keeping a Journal.

22. Music

If it is helpful, retreatants may use recorded music to deepen spiritual experiences during meditations and contemplations, and to build or maintain a mood conducive to the prayers and petitions of each Week. Ignatius was a great lover of music because it could stir the soul, but in his day the only music available was live music. Ignatius would have been delighted to know that uplifting music is now readily available to anyone at any time.

Note: Since listening to music may also be a distraction, retreatants should report to their guide how and when they are listening to music privately and how it is affecting their progress in the Exercises. (For suggestions on how to use music, see the Appendix B: How to Choose Music for Prayer.)

23. Making the Exercises in Small Groups

Traditionally, each retreatant makes the classic Spiritual Exercises in solitude and silence, talking to no one except one's spiritual guide. However, Jesus usually sent his disciples out in small teams, each member having different talents and skills. Groups making the New Spiritual Exercises may be especially helpful to each other during the process, since what God is trying to do in the world requires much teamwork as well as faith, courage, and endurance. When you are part of a team and your faith or courage begins to falter, the faith and courage of others on the team may inspire in you the strength to carry on. The same is true of the power of the team in times of intense prayer, such as a retreat, where you may need extra faith and courage to endure.

24. Forming a Prayer Team

If you enter a retreat with a group of people, it may be very beneficial to connect with two or three others and form a team, committed to encouraging and supporting each other during the retreat process. At some level, you are already a team, since you have chosen to carry out the work of Christ, each in your own way.

25. Team Meetings

If a guide is directing two or more retreatants during the same period and in the same place, it may be enriching to invite these retreatants, if they wish, to form small groups of three or four persons, to share quietly each day after the evening meal their thoughts and insights about what has been happening to them and how God has been working in them.

26. Mutual Support and Inspiration

Meetings with such a support group are not meant to take the place of a daily meeting with a well-trained spiritual guide who is to oversee and direct each one's process, nor should any group member presume to act as a spiritual director of the others. The purpose of such a group is to mutually support and encourage each other in faith, and to do this by sharing the insights and graces received since the previous meeting. This group sharing may be especially useful and profitable since each person brings different insights to the group. The sharing is also mutually inspiring since each participant gets to profit from the additional graces that the others have received.

27. Group Contemplation

From time to time, members of a sharing group may carry out an exercise, especially a contemplation, *as a group*. This is called a group contemplation. In this prayer process, all participants enter into the same contemplative moment and, in orderly fashion, continue during the prayer period to share aloud what they are experiencing, at each moment, in their imagination and what they are feeling in their heart. (For more detailed suggestions, see Appendix A: Steps in a Group Contemplation.)

Seventeen Basic Teilhardian Principles that Give Rise to the New Spiritual Exercises

The Basic Principles

1. The discoveries of modern science must form an important foundation to any contemporary spirituality if it is to be true, relevant, and inspiring.
2. Evolution is happening continually on every level of being —and it has a direction.
3. The Law of Attraction-Connection-Complexity-Consciousness is the law that is giving evolution its direction.
4. Evolution is based primarily on spirit, not on matter.
5. We all live and move and have our being in the divine milieu.
6. Everything has a "within" as well as a "without."
7. The principle of self-convergence is now operating.
8. At present, evolution is focused in the "noosphere."
9. The success of God's plan for creation depends on your conscious and creative activity to keep that divine plan evolving and developing in the direction God wants for creation.
10. Any true spirituality today must be a collective spirituality.
11. Today, even an individual spirituality, that is, a private and exclusive redemptive relationship between God and me, must include all other human beings and the rest of creation.
12. To know, love, and serve the universe with a passion.
13. To love the "invisible."
14. To love the "not-yet."
15. An evolutionary spirituality is focused primarily on grace, not on sin.
16. To recognize that union differentiates.
17. To synthesize all things in the Universal Christ.

Teilhard de Chardin is considered by many to be the most influential theologian of the twentieth century, because he was the first to integrate evolutionary science and Christian theology. In doing so, he also transformed Christian spirituality, providing fresh and powerful ways to inspire new life and new motivation in people. We are only now beginning to see the breadth and depth of the effects of his insights. In this book, I am attempting, as Teilhard put it, to "transpose" the original Ignatian Exercises into a new key, so that they now resonate with the mind, heart, and spirit of contemporary people who want to make a positive difference in their world.

If you are making the New Spiritual Exercises for the first time, please study and ponder these basic principles before beginning the formal process. During the retreat, you may come back to certain principles that may call for deeper reflection.

This book, as its title says, is about how Teilhard might have re-envisioned Ignatius' Exercises. This important section presents the foundational ideas of Teilhard's thought that influence and permeate the New Spiritual Exercises. Without understanding these basic principles, you will lose some of the energizing power of this process.

In the original Spiritual Exercises, Ignatius had no need to establish basic principles foundational to his own thought and spirituality, for his theological assumptions were much the same as those shared by almost everyone in Christian Europe at that time. These usually included a preoccupation with sin, temptations, the devil, death, fear of hell, doing penance, the agonies of Christ, and one's individual salvation.

However, the same is not true today. We are in a very different place theologically, ecologically, and especially in spirituality. For any adequate understanding of a contemporary approach to the Exercises, a new set of explanatory foundational principles is required. The ideas in this section will influence your experience of each of the following Spiritual Exercises and enrich the benefit you will receive from them.

For your benefit, at the beginning of each of the following Spiritual Exercises and in certain other places, one or more of these basic principles is noted in brackets as influencing the content of that exercise.

Principle 1: The discoveries of modern science must form an important foundation to any contemporary spirituality if it is to be true, relevant, and inspiring.

Any true spirituality must include humanity in its wholeness, as that "wholeness" is understood by any civilization in its time. For us today this wholeness must include, for example, a coherent picture of the evolution of the universe. It must spell out, as well as we can at this time, what we know of God's plan not only for humanity but also for all creation. And knowledge about that divine plan is to be found not only in scripture and tradition but also in the discoveries of science.

Modern science in its many fields—physics, biology, chemistry, geology, anthropology, psychology, sociology, genetics, astronomy, and all their various combinations—has been helping to form a coherent picture of us and our universe, and to understand its wholeness and the inextricable interconnectivity of all creation.

Creation is itself a "book" of revelation that took fourteen billion years to write, during which time God has been revealing God and God's ways to us. Teilhard would see this "book" as a companion text to the scriptures, each helping to better comprehend the other. It is mostly during the past century that scientists have learned how to begin to decipher this cosmic story. Thanks to science, we are beginning to see what Saint Paul calls, "the breadth and length and height and depth [of Christ's love for us in creation] that surpasses knowledge, so that you may be filled with all the fullness of God" (Eph 3:18–19).

For Teilhard, any new truth about the universe or the Earth that science discovers needs to be integrated into our spirituality, since that truth is bound to reveal, upon prayerful reflection, something more about who God is, who we are, and what God's plans are for us and for the rest of creation. Therefore, it will never be harmful to our faith to read and digest the facts science has discovered. Mostly, the information will be awe-inspiring and humbling, because it will reveal some new aspect of God's creative loving plan.

Faith presupposes reason and enriches it. This is a basic principle of a healthy spirituality. Science uses reason to uncover knowledge of creation. Knowledge of creation acquired through reason and enlightened by faith rises to knowledge of God. Why would we ever want to exclude knowledge discovered by science in our design of a contemporary spirituality or spiritual practice?

Principle 2: Evolution is happening continually on every level of being—and has a direction.

This principle is perhaps the most innovative of all the principles of Teilhard's spirituality. Notice, as you experience these new exercises, how pervasive and central it is to Teilhard's discernment of God's plan for humanity and for all of creation. For him, that God from the beginning created an evolving universe is a pivotal fact of divine revelation. It is a fact upon which we must base our thinking about almost everything else, including theology and spirituality.

The fact of the universality of evolution has been revealed, not by scripture or tradition, but by the most ancient cosmic "book" of revelation, creation itself. And, were it not for science, we would never know it. For spirituality, the most important facet of this revelation is that it is in the evolutionary process on all layers of being where God and Christ may be most readily found. Before the mid-nineteenth century, no scientist or spiritual writer had grasped—or could have grasped—this pivotal fact.

For Teilhard, evolution is happening not only in biology, geology, and astronomy, but in every aspect of life, individually, socially, psychologically, and spiritually. And this is why ongoing evolution everywhere must shape any spirituality that claims to be valid for our time. It is the continuous increase in complexity and consciousness that makes evolution such an important factor in the cosmic process and in our personal and collective lives.

We have only to look carefully to see that every science is evolving; every art form is evolving; transportation is evolving; communication is evolving; government is evolving; society is evolving; philosophical thought is evolving; and even theology, religion, and doctrine are evolving. Cardinal John Henry Newman, a contemporary of Charles Darwin, was a great proponent of the evolution of Christian doctrine. His ideas are spelled out in his *Essay on the Development of Christian Doctrine*, where he shows how theological truths, such as those about Christ and the people of God, can become more detailed and more richly and clearly understood over the centuries.

Individually and collectively, says Teilhard, all things are going forward and upward with a purpose that follows a central law that was originally implanted by God in every particle of the universe.

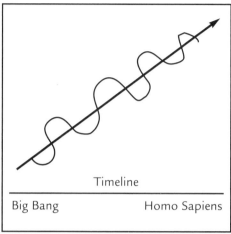

Fig. 1 The Trajectory of Evolution.
Even though the curved evolutionary path has had its ups and downs, its gains and losses, the trajectory of evolution has followed a forward and upward path.

Identifying this central law and the general "direction of evolution" are perhaps two of Teilhard's most important discoveries. Although he called this central law the Law of Complexity-Consciousness, it becomes more understandable when it is more completely named as the Law of Attraction-Connection-Complexity-Consciousness.

Principle 3: The Law of Attraction-Connection-Complexity-Consciousness is the law that is giving evolution its direction.

From the first moment after the Big Bang, as Teilhard might describe it, the elementary particles that exploded outward in all directions seemed driven to attract other particles and to bond with them (Attraction-Connection). Today's physicist might describe those first moments as a quantum field. As elementary particles in this field kept attracting each other and making connections, over time they became more and more complex particles. A glance at a chemical table summarizes the evolving story of these connections and their growing complexity (Attraction-Connection-Complexity).

All the original particles were nonorganic and nonliving, science tells us. It took billions of years for organic chemicals to appear and the laws of organic chemistry to evolve. Moreover, it took billions of years for living things to appear on Earth and the laws of biology to evolve. Such scientific laws may be seen as emergent properties of an evolving creation.

This Law of Attraction-Connection-Complexity-Consciousness has continued to operate throughout many billions of years until it eventually produced the first living things, such as single-celled bacteria. Following this law, vegetative things capable of growth and reproduction, such as plants and vines, emerged; then creatures with movement and sensation, like birds, fish, and other animals. Finally came creatures like us of such neuronal complexity that consciousness and reflective self-awareness burst forth. These were new intangible emergent properties of creation, fulfilling the Creator's evolutionary law (Attraction-Connection-Complexity-Consciousness).

Saint Paul in his letters seems fascinated by the law of connection and the ways in which more complex unities are formed (Eph 5:31–32). Paul also explores the unity of the human body and uses that unity as a metaphor for the complexity and consciousness of the Body of Christ (1 Cor 12:12–13).

According to Teilhard, we humans are currently at the tip of the arrow that reveals the direction and trajectory of evolution. That arrow tells us that God wants humans to aim toward ever-higher levels of complexity and consciousness (see fig. 1).

While technology keeps evolving at greater and greater speed, the more important question for Teilhard is how humans as a species can keep pace evolving spiritually. For example, how can the human race grow in its ability to create peace in society and among nations, promote equality, uphold justice, produce abundance for all, and be ever more generous and compassionate? Keeping the tip of that evolutionary arrow moving forward and upward becomes a primary aim of contemporary spirituality. The task is obviously up to us. It is a challenge to the human spirit working with God's grace to develop a deeper consciousness of who we are and where we ought to be going.

Defining Consciousness in the New Spiritual Exercises

It is important to remember that consciousness has two essential components: awareness and appropriate response.

In order to be conscious, it is not enough to be simply awake or aware of what is going on. To be truly conscious, you also need to respond appropriately to what you are experiencing. It requires a response to the stimulus—at least some thought or reflection. Also, in response you may choose to act or choose not to act.

Becoming conscious changes you. Suppose you have a spontaneous insight. It may be a brilliant insight, but if you do nothing with it, if you give no response to it, think no more about it, fail to share it with others, or make no choices regarding it, it is as if you never had the insight. You remain unconscious, because nothing has happened to you because of your insight. You have not claimed it or owned it. You have done nothing with it.

For Teilhard, an important element in spiritual practice is to keep developing your consciousness, so that you can wake up to and act on what is truly real. He invites you to learn to "see" the way he sees reality, with spiritual eyes. Saint Paul calls them "your inward eyes" or "the eyes of your heart" (Eph 1:18). When you wake up each morning, you see things with your physical eyes thanks to the light of the sun. When you wake up spiritually, you become conscious. You see things with new eyes thanks to the light of Christ. In the words of the popular hymn, we pray, "Christ, be our light!"

Saint Paul says that as we learn to live consciously in Christ, our perception of reality changes. "When anyone is united in Christ, that person has become a new creature; the old life is over; a new life has already begun" (a free translation of 2 Cor 5:17). Paul is describing a state of consciousness that he has personally experienced, where everything has become new for him. In that state, you begin to see yourself and everything else surrounded by God's love, and you realize that at any moment your spirit can be present in any part of that

19

vast and cosmic divine reality you wish to be. This state might be described as Christ-consciousness. In it, you discover that your true self in Christ is as unfettered as light.

That same God-consciousness embodied in the human Jesus is present in all of us, individually and collectively, though many of us may have not "awakened" to it yet. It is present and waits to be awakened. "The day of my spiritual awakening," wrote Mechtild of Magdeburg (1210–1280), "was the day I saw—and knew I saw—all things in God and God in all things."

Even though you or I may not have reached Mechtild's enviable state of awareness, we still live in Christ and united to Christ. We still live in the divine milieu, unconditionally loved by God. Our faith gives us that assurance. Nevertheless, we are invited to grow and evolve into that state of Christ-consciousness where we can see reality with new eyes, the eyes of Christ.

Ignatius wants the retreatant to attain that special state of consciousness, to see with the eyes of Christ. That is why he has retreatants meditate on the events of Christ's life. He wants us to get inside Jesus, to become so immersed in the thoughts, words, emotions, and actions of Jesus that we know what it is to think and live like Jesus. Paul asks us to "put on the mind of Christ Jesus" for our own times. For example, in the mind of Jesus, there is no separation between Jesus' thoughts and God's thoughts, and no separation between what Jesus does and what God wants him to do. That's quite an ideal! Yet even for us, within the circumstances of each new day, our consciousness rooted in Christ calls us to appropriate responses and appropriate action.

Principle 4: Evolution is based primarily on spirit, not on matter.

Teilhard relies on theology to help him explain this basic principle, which asserts that in the beginning was spirit. On the other hand, many scientists would assume the opposite, namely, that at the beginning of space-time there was only matter (or a quantum field). Such scientists might say, "From the Big Bang there came nothing but material particles or fields of energy."

Everything in Teilhard's thought, however, is based on the fundamental theological belief that spirit is what started it all. Our loving

Creator God, pure spirit, wanted to express the divine self outside the divine self, as it were. Teilhard would suggest that this divine loving self-expression took its original form as what we now call the Big Bang.

If you prefer the theological version of John the Evangelist, "In the beginning was the Word…" and creation came about because God spoke a creative Word. That divine Word, when spoken, was filled with the Holy Spirit, and as Spirit it gave life and meaning to every particle of matter and quantum field of energy. God's Spirit gave existence to creation and continues to keep it in existence from moment to moment (John 1:1 ff).

When Teilhard uses the word *spirit*, he is not referring exclusively to the divine spirit, but also to the human spirit.

From various writings of Teilhard, one can build a picture of how he saw the relationship between *spirit* (divine and human) and *matter* (the physical world). Among other things, he said:

> *Spirit is the origin and term of evolution.* Spirit created matter, remains with it and within it, sustains it and will bring it to its complete fulfillment.
>
> *Spirit is the power of unity scattered throughout the fragments of the universe.* Spirit, working in matter through the Law of Attraction-Connection-Complexity-Consciousness, is the unifying force in creation, bringing all the elements of creation to ever-higher levels of unity or oneness.
>
> *Spirit is the force driving everything toward synthesis and sublimation*, that is, toward higher levels of existence. Spirit explains why everything in the physical world is evolving.
>
> *Spirit is continually leading the universe toward some more spiritual state.* For Teilhard, Jesus is inviting us to join with him in performing his greatest miracle of all, that of transforming the world once again, this time with the evolutionary power of love.
>
> *Spirit is personal, not some abstract or impersonal force such as gravity or electromagnetism.* For Teilhard, the Holy Spirit is a divine person and, as such, wants to inspire us, individually and collectively, to create a world reborn in God-consciousness.

Principle 5: We all live and move and have our being in the divine milieu.

All spiritualities must deal with questions like: How does God fit into my life? Where is God in relation to me? How do I picture God?

Tradition offers two standard ways to think about God and "where" God is.

The first says that God is *transcendent*. In its most popular interpretation, *transcendent* means that God is far away from me, elsewhere, remote, in heaven. So, when I pray or think about God from this perspective, I lift up my eyes and address God, sending my praise or petition skyward to the throne of God. "Our Father, who art in heaven...." *Transcendence*, however, in its fullest theological sense means "otherness," which is not the same as remoteness. God is totally other, that is, there is nothing to which to compare God.

The second traditional way of relating to God says that God is *immanent*, that God dwells inside me, as close to me as my own heart. When I pray from this approach, I go into the deepest recesses of myself and meet God there. This perspective is especially useful during the time after receiving Eucharist and during periods of meditation.

Theologically, the transcendence and immanence of God are correlative terms, and indeed, most believers find no difficulty in relating to a God who is both transcendent and immanent.

Teilhard does not try to dissuade you from using either or both of these approaches—God as transcendent and God as immanent—but he prefers a third way. He says that from the first moment of creation, God has been present to everything, keeping everything in being. He emphasizes the omnipresence of God. For Teilhard, the way God does this is by creating a *divine milieu* in which everything that exists lives and moves, and has its being.

At all times, we live in this divine milieu much like fish swimming in the milieu of water. Fish do not focus on the water that surrounds and permeates them. They go through life mostly unaware of it, even though they live and move and have their being in it. They do not notice it. Nor do we notice the invisible air surrounding us that we take in with every breath and in which we live and move and enjoy life—and could not live without.

It is much the same for us in the spiritual realm. Even though we live and move and have our being in this divine milieu, we go through life mostly unaware of it. Teilhard would like us to begin becoming aware of this divine milieu and begin to "see" it everywhere. It makes all of us one and keeps all of us one, yet allows every element of creation to maintain its unique individuality. We all maintain our individuality, yet we are never isolated from each other because we are all part of the organically integrated whole, created and nourished by the divine milieu.

God's presence is always at your fingertips. No matter what you touch—your toothbrush, your coffee cup, your pen, your computer keyboard, your car keys, a coin in your pocket—that thing exists in the divine milieu. Everything you touch, see, hear, or taste is being kept in being by God's Spirit. Each thing is part of that great integrated whole. That is why Jesus could say that God knows and has counted every hair on your head.

Even intangible things like your thoughts, wishes, and worries are living in the divine milieu. Nothing that exists can be outside the divine milieu. You are never an isolated being. You are always connected to everything else in the divine milieu.

Saint Ignatius in his Spiritual Exercises taught Teilhard that he was to learn to find God in all things. With this concept of the divine milieu, Teilhard takes Ignatius' "finding God in all things" to the next level. And he tells us how we can do it.

Principle 6: Everything has a "within" as well as a "without."

Obviously, every physical thing has what Teilhard calls a "without," that is, an outward appearance, qualities that can be measured by scientific tools—color, shape, size, weight, texture, temperature, density, strength, movement, and so on. But what is new in this principle is that everything that has a without also has a "within." Of course, God has a within, an unfathomable one (Isa 55:8–9).

Nor would anyone challenge that each person has an inner life—a within—that cannot be reduced to something that science can look at in a microscope or measure with a ruler. Your within is certainly different from any or all of the roles you may play in life.

23

Even if you were to be stripped of every name, social identity, function, position, employment, nationality, talent, and skill, there would still be a "you," namely, your within (see Psalm 139:1–4). Your within might include your knowledge, your beliefs, your values, your loves, your appreciation of beauty, your creative ideas, your memories, your longings, your fears, the songs you know, and so on. Every human being has an immense within.

From this principle, Teilhard wants us to see that everything, including plants, trees, rocks, lakes, moons, and planets, also has a within, a unique identity given to each one by God. Each plant and flower in your garden has a unique identity and history that are part of its within.

But Teilhard goes far beyond this. For him, every atom and molecule of the universe is unique, is held in being by Spirit, and has its unique fourteen-billion-year history, starting from the first moment. Theoretically at least, each of the trillions of cells in your body today could trace the ancestry of each of their elements back to the first moment of creation. Each particular particle's story is known and held in God's mind by Spirit—how it made connection to another specific particle in those early moments of creation to form the first atom. God would know the story of the first time this original particle became part of a molecule of a primitive gas, and so on, all through that particle's fourteen-billion-year history. Perhaps that particle today is a part of your body or is in the body of someone you love.

In his spirituality, Teilhard wants you to learn to "see" the within of each thing, especially the inner life of each person. Using Teilhard's expression, Ignatius in the Spiritual Exercises wanted each retreatant to attempt to imagine the within of Jesus of Nazareth, the within of Mary, and the within of the Creator.

Principle 7: The principle of self-convergence is now operating.

Self-convergence refers to a kind of self-integrating process. It is an evolutionary ability you possess to make yourself more whole and integral—a way of putting your life together. It is a process of inward evolution or "involution." In other words, you possess the continuing ability to find ways to reconfigure, simplify, and integrate the growing complexity and consciousness that is you. You can find ways to integrate into yourself all the thousands of new inputs that are daily coming in from our rapidly changing and increasingly complex society.

For example, now you are reading this book. You are taking its ideas into your mind, comparing them, making judgments about them, seeing how they fit with your experience and with your faith, welcoming them or modifying them. Your experience with them and response to them are being integrated or converged into who you are. While making the New Spiritual Exercises you will be continually challenged to do much self-converging. Do it with consciousness.

Principle 8: At present, evolution is focused in the "noosphere."

Although, over long periods of time, biological adaptation and evolution continue to be recognized in all living species—even homo sapiens—evolution today is happening primarily—and quickly accelerating—in the growth of human knowledge and consciousness. Worldwide, we are enveloped in ideas, information, knowledge, wisdom, goals, purposes, and powerful feelings, just as we are all enveloped in Earth's atmosphere. Teilhard called this envelope of information, thought, and emotions the *noosphere*.

Roughly speaking, the noosphere might be called the collective mind and heart of the planet, or humanity's psyche. Whatever is in the noosphere remains a source of knowledge and love accessible to any individual, though it took all of humanity to create it. And humanity keeps enriching it.

We can see the evidence for noospheric evolution, not only in the tremendous continuing growth in information and knowledge, but also in the evolutionary development of our growing capacity for cooperative and caring interpersonal connections—even though many choose not to use this capacity. Nevertheless, this development shows the real possibility of humankind as a whole coming to ever-higher consciousness through higher and more complex social unions—even sharing contemplative moments.

The arrow of evolution, currently working in the noosphere, is leading us worldwide toward a common outlook and a common hope. Eventually, Teilhard envisions, the noosphere will constitute a single thinking-loving system "in which each person sees, feels, desires and suffers for itself the same things as all the others at the same time" (*Phenomenon* no. 251).

For Teilhard, the noosphere is the natural and necessary underlying structure for the supernatural (and what some have called the "hyperpersonal") Body of Christ. As the noosphere gradually is correctly perceived for what it is destined to be, it will help humanity create a personal and personalizing world in which the value of the individual is not only preserved but also enhanced. Although humanity as a whole may be far from that ideal state at present, the task facing us is quite clear. According to Teilhard, the Body of Christ is meant to become an "organized super-aggregation of loving souls." For Teilhard, this image is another way to describe the aim of God's plan for creation, the Christ Project.

Principle 9: The success of God's plan for creation depends on your conscious and creative activity to keep that divine plan evolving and developing in the direction God wants for creation.

In the past, no one even imagined that there was some great divine evolutionary plan for creation in which humans were meant to participate as co-creators during their lives on Earth. For centuries, many Christians saw their earthly days as merely a behavioral test for entry into heaven; Earth served merely as their classroom where they prepared for their final exam and hoped to graduate into heaven. For them, their daily activity and professional work did not build the kingdom of God on Earth, but simply generated in the end a scorecard of good and bad behavior. They believed they would be judged worthy of a place in heaven based simply on the final grade they achieved on this test of good and bad deeds.

For Teilhard, in contrast, the Christ Project is why God created the evolving universe in the first place. Up to the advent of the human species, no creature was capable of grasping the idea of this great divine project and how it works. In addition, it took the revelations of Jesus Christ plus twenty centuries of theological reflection and centuries of scientific discoveries to tie things all together to begin to identify the grand divine project and the evolutionary law governing it.

The plan is not only that each human being would be "saved" individually, but also that we humans, working together as one family, would consciously cooperate in the creative work of this Universal Being. We are invited to be an integral part of that project. Some participate in it consciously and creatively. Many others, like research scientists and people in the helping professions, cooperate in it, too, even though they may be unaware of the Christ Project by name.

Principle 10: Any true spirituality today must be a collective spirituality.

Most spiritual traditions offer an individualized form of spirituality, one that primarily nurtures a relationship between you and God. They present a path that emphasizes personal sin and salvation—"saving my soul"—and union with God. For this reason, most people, certainly Christians, have been focusing their spiritual lives on their personal salvation and on helping save the individual souls of others. From an evolutionary perspective, however, this is not enough.

The evolving noosphere, which is the collective mind and heart of the planet, calls for a collective spirituality, one in which people, individually and collectively, create and contribute to its evolution. The purpose of such a relational spirituality is to bring the noosphere to its highest level of convergence, eventually operating as a single consciousness. This convergent oneness of humanity and the planet will be a knowledge-based and love-inspired union and communion. Only in this collective way may we create an adequate infrastructure for the full emergence of Christ as a Cosmic Christ (1 Cor 6:15, 17, 19). In this perspective, when Jesus says, "The Kingdom of God is among you," it would mean, in Teilhard's language, that the divine project is already under way.

Teilhard believed that those who grasped this idea would feel the call to spend their energies not only on their own personal salvation but, with their eyes focused on the vision of humanity as a whole, would put their minds, hearts, and energy into building the great Body of Christ.

More specifically, they would realize that a major task of any true contemporary spirituality should be to help prepare the collective mind and heart of the planet for the Cosmic Christ. This is the Christ Project. Helping achieve this convergent oneness of humanity by promoting further evolution will demand that each person learn the creative art of imagining a better future and helping make it happen—over and over. The fundamental choice to help achieve this convergent oneness would naturally form an important part of any spirituality today.

Principle 11: Today, even an individual spirituality, that is, a private and exclusive redemptive relationship between God and me, must include all other human beings and the rest of creation.

We are all joined to each other for the success or failure of the divine project. We are all one species. Whatever happens to a fellow human somehow affects me. I cannot live my life as if my spirituality is something just between God and me.

Teilhard is not saying you should not have a personal prayer life. What he is saying is that spirituality must include awareness of and cooperation with God's unfinished project, that is, building the body of the Universal Christ. Each person has work to do as part of this grand project. Your work is connected to the efforts of all other persons, so it is part of your work to support and encourage others, since the success of your part of the great project often depends on the success of their parts.

For Teilhard, you are not the center of your life purpose. The Christ Project is.

Principle 12: To know, love, and serve the universe with a passion.

You may notice that this Teilhardian principle, taken directly from his book *The Divine Milieu*, turns the first principle of traditional spirituality on its head. Traditionally, we were told that our first commitment was to know, love, and serve God with all our heart, soul, mind, and strength; in other words, to love God with a passion.

It was, at least, strongly suggested that loving things of the world could lead us away from that primary love of God.

Without denying the primacy of loving God passionately, Teilhard also invites us to love the cosmos—all of creation—with a passion. For him, that is where spirituality must begin—with the tangible awesome beauty and unity of creation and the needs of that creation.

However, Teilhard is not saying we should love creation the same way we love God. Our love for God is primarily a *responsive love*, since God has first loved us. As we become aware of God's love for us and its unconditional depths, we respond to it. Our love for God is a receptive and responsive experience.

Our love for the created world is quite different. Teilhard asks us to love creation with a *generative love*, a love that wants to produce something new with the materials that surround us. Creation is something that waits to be continually re-created. It needs us to re-create it. It needs our human spirit to imagine what that transformation will be. It needs us to love it generatively into being.

Every creative person knows this kind of generative love. The painter loves the painting before it reaches the canvas. The composer loves the song before its notes are written on the staff or played on the keyboard. The researcher loves the life-saving drug he or she is searching for even before its chemical structure is successfully deciphered. Parents love their child before it is conceived. This is generative love. It gives existence to what did not exist before.

But both responsive love and generative love flow together. Teilhard's assumption is that God has been revealing himself to us for almost fourteen billion years with divine expressions of generative love. To study creation introduces us to God and the generative ways God loves us. Creation is our first lesson in learning about who God is. Learning to love what God created is to learn about God. The more passionately we come to know, love, and serve the universe and its God-given purpose, the more passionately we can come to know and love God. As we respond to the generative love of God seen in creation, we are inspired to love it generatively, too. The world—the cosmos—is not the enemy of God or the antithesis of God, but the gateway to God. In creation, God's Spirit is continually being made manifest to us.

In *The Divine Milieu*, Teilhard wrote, "God is as pervasive and perceptible as the atmosphere in which we are bathed. What prevents you from enfolding him in your arms? Only one thing—your inability to see him" (pp. 45–6).

Principle 13: To love the "invisible."

Like Basic Principle 6, this principle encourages you to get in touch with your inner self, your invisible "within." Learning to love the invisible is the condition for successful growth in the divine milieu. Within you is the spark of the divine Spirit that is pushing you to create and evolve, to apply in your own life the Law of Attraction-Connection-Complexity-Consciousness.

This principle also reminds you that there are more things in your life that are invisible and intangible than those that are visible and tangible. This is part of Teilhard's wish that we could all learn to "see" the invisible the way he sees it.

For example, when two people deeply in love get married, they create a new intangible being that we call their "marriage." That marriage-being enjoys a life of its own, almost independently of the two partners. The marriage has its own story, its own personality, and its own spirit. The marriage can be sick or weak—people refer to their marriage as "on the rocks"—while the partners individually are healthy and strong. Or the marriage can be quite healthy while the partners may be sick, physically or mentally.

What is important to recognize in this example is that the "marriage" is invisible. One cannot see the "marriage" with one's physical eyes; one can see only the husband and wife and their words and actions. Yet this invisible entity, this relationship, has a powerful effect on many people. Teilhard wants you to learn to see, love, and nurture these invisible realities.

A team is an invisible reality as well as a visible one. Think about it. If a certain sports team is one of your favorite teams, you love the team, not simply the individual athletes. You love the team as a separate entity. The players may change from month to month and year to year, but the team remains. To truly see things like "teams," "interactions," and "team spirit," you need new eyes, eyes that have learned to see the invisible.

Teilhard wrote in *The Divine Milieu*, "Throughout my life, by means of my life, the world has little by little caught fire in my sight until, aflame all around me, it has become almost completely luminous from within" (p. 46).

Principle 14: To love the "not-yet."

An evolutionary spirituality is always about striving toward the future that has yet to become manifest, to extend evolution's arrow toward ever-higher levels of complexity and consciousness. Evolution is all about the future, what is yet to become, yet can only be imagined.

With the appearance of humanity on Earth, evolution developed a new dimension or expression. Evolution is no longer primarily about problem solving, adaptation, or natural selection; it is about us imagining a desired future, while living in the present and very aware of the current state of things, and choosing to create that desired future. The purpose of an evolutionary spirituality is to teach people how to envision the future that God envisions for creation and to choose to bring it about. It is summed up in the not-yet question you may ask yourself each year and each day: "What will I make my life about?"

The best science fiction writers are completely absorbed in imagining the "not-yet," in what will eventually be discovered by science and created by technology, in how individuals and society will grow and develop. Research scientists, by definition, are searching for something that has not yet been invented. Paleontologists, like Teilhard, are always hoping they will discover some fossils that have not yet been found. What parent has not looked lovingly upon a child and imagined for it a wonderful "not-yet"?

Recall all the things you have outgrown, left behind, or given up so that you would be able to create the future you envisioned, your personal not-yet. What is it in your imagined future that you can love enough, generatively, that you are willing to do whatever it takes to bring it about?

In the fundamental structure of the Hebrew Scriptures and Hebrew spirituality is a focus on the not-yet. For Adam, for Noah, for Abraham, for Moses, God is always out ahead, making promises that have yet to happen, and calling for faith that those promises will be fulfilled in some evolutionary future. Jesus, too, lived out this same "not-yet" spirituality during his time on Earth.

The night before his passion, while eating supper with his friends, Jesus talked mostly about the "not-yet," what was to happen in the future to him and to his friends. In this most poignant moment, Jesus' thoughts were focused not on his immanent suffering and death but on what lay beyond. Jesus was always envisioning what he desired to create, and choosing it. This is why the "not-yet" is so important to Teilhard. The "not-yet" is a central focus in an evolutionary spirituality.

Principle 15: An evolutionary spirituality is focused primarily on grace, not on sin.

Traditional spirituality often places a spotlight on an individual's personal sins, the importance of recalling those sins and doing reparation for them and, when possible, resolving them. This sometimes is referred to as sin/redemption spirituality. Yet, in contrast, it is difficult to find an instance of Jesus asking people to enumerate their sins or do reparation for them. Instead, he quickly forgave the sins of those who trusted in him. Why? Because he was more interested in having the person return to the community, spiritually unencumbered and free to be loving and productive there. For Jesus, each person had important work to do for God and needed to be free within to do it.

This forgiving attitude toward sin is an often-unnoticed point in the parable of the prodigal son. The loving father never asks the prodigal to do penance or reparation for his sins. He never asks for the return of the squandered inheritance. As soon as they meet, the son begins to report his sins and even enumerate them, but the father will hear none of it. Those sins and wasted years are swept out of the way in the father's transcending love and forgiveness. Without any questions or inquiry, the father simply reinstates the son as a full and respected member of the family, so that the son can freely carry on the work he was meant to do. The central fact of their first meeting is the welcoming gift, or grace, that the father gives the returning son. It is God's gift to each of us to see oneself as a full and respected member of God's family.

This is the grace of *metanoia* (a change in thinking and behavior with a future orientation, not with a focus on past failures and sins) that the father offers and that comes as such a total surprise to his prodigal son. God's unconditional divine grace often comes as a total surprise also to us, who have been taught to focus on our sinfulness. But *metanoia* with a future orientation is very clearly what the Father wants, according to Jesus.

Simply stated, divine grace transcends sin. In the language of the Christ Project, the father might be saying to the prodigal, "Let's not focus on the past, my son. Stay focused on my love and my grace. Never let others discourage you concerning your past. There is much work to be done in the present and the future, and you can best do your part of that work as my forward-looking, free son. Most important to me is our work together that waits to be done. And I want you to do it at my side, in joyful union with me, basking in my unconditional love."

With God's forgiving grace, we are renewed again, made whole. No matter what our past has been, we are given another chance to create our lives the way God and we truly want.

Notice that this divine gift to move forward does not require completely resolving all the issues of the past. That is work the father (God) assumes. The father does not tell the prodigal son to go out and resolve all the difficult issues with his older brother. It is the father who goes out to the field and assumes the responsibility for initiating the reconciliation process. He knows that for their success they must all learn to work together as a family.

Principle 16: To recognize that union differentiates.

For many, this "law of union" is one of the hardest insights of Teilhard to grasp, but it is very powerful. It says that the more completely you give yourself to creating union (in togetherness, friendship, marriage, family, teamwork), the more clearly your own identity is clarified. You won't discover yourself by staying away from people or by just comparing and contrasting yourself with them, but by becoming partners with them. You learn who you truly are by making connections, for example, building friendships, getting married, playing in teams, joining a workplace team, and contributing to and cooperating in these relationships and groups with all your heart and skill.

Teilhard spells out this "law of union" very clearly. The law that "union differentiates" states that while participating in any "organized whole the parts perfect themselves and fulfill themselves."

A well-organized whole is a union (for example, a friendship, marriage, or team) that has a genuine and intrinsic life of its own. The members of such a union are not random parts, just as your hand is not a random protuberance on your body. Your hand is an integral member of the organic whole that is your body. It has specific abilities and purposes within that body. It is a highly differentiated individual member that enjoys its uniqueness, differentiation, and perfection precisely when it functions as part of the whole. In a similar way, you experience your uniqueness and highest capacities precisely when you function as part of a greater whole. With your hand, the whole of you can write a letter. If you cut off your arm and put a pen between your fingers, that arm cannot write a letter. It is always the parts interacting in relationship to the whole that accomplishes things. The point is that the abilities of your hand are best identified and differentiated when your hand remains in complete cooperative union with your body.

Relationships always bring complexity. You learn who you truly are by making your life more complex. And with complexity, as you welcome it, comes consciousness—among other things, a growing consciousness of your true identity and your capacities, more of your wholeness.

Principle 17: To synthesize all things in the Universal Christ.

This is another perspective related to the principle of self-convergence (Basic Principle 7). Once you learn to see with Teilhard's new eyes, you begin to realize that everything you do is being done not only by you but also by Christ in whom you live and move and have your being. If your hand had its own self-awareness, it would realize that everything it does is being done, not only by itself, but also by you, the whole person in whom the hand lives and moves and has its being. It is in Christ that the universe in general converges upon itself, as more and more people become conscious of this universal self-convergence process.

When most of the human cells in the Cosmic Christ become aware not only of their own identity and work but also of their larger identity and work as part of Christ's Body, then the Christ Project will be approaching its fulfillment. The members will not only be a part of the Cosmic Christ, as they have always been, but now they will know it.

For Teilhard, Christ is the Divine Milieu. He got the insight from St. Paul:

> He [Jesus Christ] is the image of the invisible God, the first-born of all creatures. In him everything in heaven and on earth was created, things visible and invisible…all were created through him and for him. He existed before all else that is. In him everything continues in being. It is he who is head of the body, the church; he is the source of the body's life, the first-born of the dead, so that he may be first in everything. It pleased God to make absolute fullness [of divine nature] reside in him (Col 1:15–19).

One area where this self-convergence of human cells in the Cosmic Body has been happening is with communication. Primitive humans could communicate only face to face. Once humanity learned to write, people could communicate by sending letters to each other. With e-mail today, one can instantly send an identical message to hundreds of people scattered all over the Earth. This is global self-convergence. It is the inevitable result of the evolutionary Law of Attraction-Connection-Complexity-Consciousness. If Teilhard were alive today, he would affirm that the Internet has become part of the universal Body of Christ. Humanity still has a ways to go, since currently, at times, the Internet is being used to devolve rather than evolve humanity, to separate and divide people rather than unify them. But Teilhard is optimistic that we will eventually learn the way of love.

The First Week

The Presence of God

Ignatius recommends that before each spiritual exercise you become consciously aware that you are immersed in the presence of God. Although in fact you cannot escape the presence of God, you can easily "forget" that you are kept alive from moment to moment in that divine presence, the divine milieu.

Take a few moments—or as long as you need—to realize that you are going to spend time with someone who loves you. This is not about you trying to find God. Ignatius turns that idea around. He says, "I am to imagine how God our Lord is looking in wonder at me" (75). He is suggesting that you are to picture God right here looking at you, as you might look with delight and admiration at your own child. If I knew that God was looking at me with delight and admiration as I enter a period of prayer, I think there would be a smile on my lips and a glow in my heart, realizing that God loves me that much.

In the beginning, some newer retreatants may require some help recalling God's presence. After a while, it should become much simpler and easier. Here are a few imagination suggestions to get started. Use whatever you find helpful.

- Imagine yourself immersed in the divine milieu (as in an immense light) with the divine light surrounding you and flowing through every cell of your body.
- Picture yourself as a cell in some organ or body part of the cosmic Body of Christ.
- Picture Jesus (at any age you wish) standing beside you, eager to be with you, lovingly energizing and supporting your prayer.

- Picture yourself surrounded by the clear bright light of the Holy Spirit, perhaps in the shape of a huge, protective, grace-filled bubble of light.
- Repeat a simple prayer silently with each exhaled breath, such as, "Come, Lord Jesus" or "Abba, I know you are here."

The Way God Loves

One of the most memorable experiences of the original Spiritual Exercises is its final exercise. In Latin, it is commonly referred to as the *Contemplatio ad Amorem*. In this experience, Ignatius offers a way to learn how to "reach for" and, it is hoped, "attain" the ability *to love the way God loves*. We learn how to love by watching how God loves us.

Teilhard's entire spirituality begins with the *Contemplatio* and he develops it to new heights. His book, *The Divine Milieu*, can be summed up as a spirituality that shows us, as Ignatius would say, how "to find God in all things." So, in these New Spiritual Exercises, we also begin—and end, as Ignatius does—with the *Contemplatio*.

Beginning the retreat with this exercise immediately immerses retreatants into their existing loving relationship with God and creation.

Two Spiritual Truths

In his introduction to this contemplation, Ignatius wants us to be mindful of two important spiritual truths about love, which are still true today. In Ignatius' words:

> The first [spiritual truth] is that love ought to manifest itself more by deeds than by words (230).
>
> The second [spiritual truth] is that love consists in mutual communication between the two persons. That is, the one who loves gives and communicates to the beloved what he or she has, or a part of what one has or can have; and the beloved in return does the same to the lover. Thus, if one has knowledge, one gives it to the other who does not; and similarly in regard to honors and riches. Each shares with the other (231).

What Ignatius is describing here is the way God, as Lover, loves. God's loving is an unconditionally generous sharing with all that he loves. And the sharing is done in deeds, not just in words.

Four Developmental Stages

In the four "points" of this contemplation, Ignatius notes four evolving stages for us to observe the ways God expresses love for us. These are for us to reflect upon, delight in, be grateful for, stand in awe of, and, we hope, practice:

> In the first stage, *giving gifts*, God gives tangible objects to us.
>
> In the second stage, *presence*, God remains at our side along with the gifts given.
>
> In the third stage, *cooperative interaction*, God keeps acting through those gifts with us and for us.
>
> In the fourth stage, *mutual indwelling*, the most evolved form of loving, God shares the divine Self (the ultimate gift) with us. In this way, God enables us (God and me) to act as one, I in God and God in me.

Notice that there is a developmental gradation or evolution in the four stages of giving or loving. Thus, instead of calling them four "points," they are more accurately four "stages" since each stage clearly advances beyond the stage before it; yet the stages are cumulative, since each subsequent stage includes the stage(s) before it.

Learning to Love the Way God Loves: Contemplation

First Prelude: From the scriptures, we learn that God chose to express the divine Self outside Itself, as it were, by creating a universe that would reflect God's creative love. From science, we learn that what came about from God's self-expression was a universe that God could delight in as it grew and evolved over many billions of years. God delighted as the human race emerged from the evolving Earth, for they would be a people who could become conscious of how much God loves them.

Second Prelude: Here imagine yourself surrounded by an omnipresent God holding the human race in loving existence and wanting to be lovingly involved with them, giving countless gifts to people, individually and collectively.

Third Prelude: Here ask for the grace to discover the thousands of ways that God loves you and all of creation; the grace to experience in your body and soul what it feels like to be loved so uniquely and unconditionally by God; the grace to feel tangibly connected to God, to be immersed in God and in God's creation; and the grace to feel deep gratitude and wonder at the boundless love God shows in every moment.

1. THE FIRST STAGE OF LOVING: GIVING GIFTS

At the first stage of the *Contemplatio*, Ignatius tells us, God gives gifts. Love is shown in action. Giving gifts is an action. It is more than words. All of creation is God's gift to us. Creation is the Original Blessing.

Note: This point and the subsequent three points may be developed in seven areas suggested below. Do not be in a hurry to cover all seven areas. If you find your gratitude and wonder naturally flowing in response to one or other areas of the divine gifts, stay with that feeling. You may spend the entire time allotted for this first contemplation in a single area.

You may come back to this exercise again and again during this day and later in your retreat. The *Contemplatio* is the summary and summit of Ignatius' Spiritual Exercises as well as of the New Spiritual Exercises. The graces flowing from this exercise can never be exhausted.

Here are the seven areas:

1. Consider the divine *gifts of creation that astronomy has revealed to us*—including gifts that Ignatius in his day had little or no awareness of or of how and when they were given. For example, Ignatius had no sense of the vast number of galaxies or the age of the universe (Basic Principle 1).

2. Observe the gifts God has been giving us that the life sciences have revealed to us. Notice that these gifts are not static, *but active, interactive, and evolving.* As life forms kept evolving in complexity over eons of time—from sensation to perception to movement to social life—we observed that consciousness became an emergent property of life. And still the evolutionary process keeps moving onward (Basic Principle 2).

3. Recognize the *evolutionary law* at work in all things. Even Saint Paul recognized that divine creation is still incomplete (see Eph 1:10, Col 2:19), still in process. Through discoveries in science and technology, we have come to recognize, in our limited way, the fundamental law driving creation onward and upward (see, for example, Paul's speech in Acts 17:22–31) (Basic Principle 14).

4. God's gifts on the *microscopic side*, revealed by science, show the incredible complexity and activity of each living being—the human genome, the trillions of cells that live in our bodies, each cell itself a living being with its own highly complex intra-active life (Basic Principle 13).

5. Recognize God's *gift of Earth itself*, our home planet. All the beauties of mountains, plains, and skies. All the power of tornadoes, hurricanes, tidal waves, floods, deserts, and frozen tundra (Basic Principle 5).

6. Do not forget to reflect on God's *gifts that flow naturally from human consciousness* and human society such as civilization, music, art, literature, society, communication, transportation, recreation, science, mathematics, architecture, ecology, entertainment, film, radio, television, etc. (Basic Principle 8).

7. Consider all the *gifts you have personally received*—talents, skills, education, opportunities, family, friends. Don't forget your five senses, as well as your memory, intelligence, willpower, imagination, freedom to choose, the ability to love and make commitments, the ability to accomplish things, to create things that never existed before, to build teams, to worship, etc. (Basic Principle 8).

After you have contemplated and reflected upon all of God's gifts, you are invited to reply to the Divine Giver in a colloquy, or personal conversation, with God. You will be asked to have a colloquy after each of the four points of this contemplation.

Colloquy: Now that you have seen the myriad gifts God has given you and your fellow humans, you are invited to show that you have felt and grasped this first level of love. You might say something like:

I stand in wonder and gratitude at the number and immensity of the gifts you have given to me and to all creation. I am also one of your gifts. It would have been so easy for me not to have been born, never to have been conceived. And here I am, uniquely loved by you. Even before I existed, you knew me by name. Give me the grace to love you and your gifts, and that is enough for me.

2. THE SECOND STAGE OF LOVING: PRESENCE

At the second stage, where the lover is present to the gifts, Ignatius suggests you contemplate how God is present to and is at the side of each element of God's creation, including you. You are both gift and recipient of the gift, and God is beside you at all times (Basic Principle 15).

After you spend time reflecting on God's loving presence alongside and in each of God's gifts—using each of the seven areas of the gifts described in the First Point—you can formulate a response appropriate to this experience of *loving presence*. Perhaps, such a second-stage prayer, emphasizing presence, might go something like this:

Just as you, God, remain present to your gifts and just as you remain at my side, I choose to respect your presence in those gifts by not wasting them or disregarding them or never using them, but by gratefully rejoicing in using them. In my loving of you, I wish also to remain present to you. To do this, I beg the grace to remain conscious that you are always at my side.

3. THE THIRD STAGE OF LOVING: COOPERATIVE INTERACTION

The third stage of loving focuses on not just presence but *personal and active interaction*. In Ignatius' words:

I will consider how God labors and works for me in all the creatures on the face of the earth; that is, he acts in the manner of one who is laboring. For example, he is working in the heavens, elements, plants, fruits, cattle, and all the rest—giving them their existence, conserving them, concurring with the vegetative and sensitive activities, and so forth (236).

Thus, God keeps acting in and through each of those seven areas of gifts (listed in the First Point). God doesn't just act once and then stop. God continues acting and interacting at every moment with, in, and through the gifts God gives in creation. And by that continuous action, creation grows and develops; it becomes more complex and continues to evolve in consciousness (Basic Principle 9).

So, for us to learn to love in the same interactive way, we will want to continue acting and interacting with the gifts we already possess and the gifts continually being given to us, so as to help creation to grow and evolve in complexity and consciousness (Basic Principle 16).

This third stage of loving again invites a new level of a prayer, one that responds in wonder and gratitude to God's interactive commitment. It might take a form something like:

> Ever-creating God in whose love I live, in reflecting on your almost fourteen billion years of divine revelation and original blessing, I have come to recognize the Law of Attraction-Connection-Complexity-Consciousness that you have placed in me and in every particle of matter you created, and that this law is designed to culminate in the spiritual transformation of all matter. I stand in wonder and awe at all this. My heart is filled with gratitude that I am one of those enjoying the privilege of recognizing, understanding, and feeling your love.

4. THE FOURTH STAGE OF LOVING: MUTUAL INDWELLING

In the fourth stage, God shares the divine Self (the ultimate gift) with the beloved, including divine qualities of justice, goodness, piety, mercy, and so forth. God does not only give gifts that are external to God, as it were, but reveals God's very self to us as an active, involved, interactive personal presence—just as the sun's rays give us the sun itself, says Ignatius, and through its rays it is an active and interactive presence (Basic Principle 5).

The physical incarnation of the divine Word in becoming a human being is one way God shared the divine Self and demonstrates this fourth stage of loving. Christ's mystical incarnation in the Eucharist is another primary expression of this self-giving of God to us. In the Universal Christ, a third expression, we are offered a way to reciprocate this self-giving kind of love, so that with Saint Paul at the fourth stage of this contemplation, we can one day say, "I no longer live, but I am alive in Christ" (Gal 2:20).

At the fourth stage of showing love, we are invited to live our day and our destiny within the Universal Christ. I live and act in God and God lives and acts in me; we act as one. Each of us lives out our day within and alongside our loving God. Also, we act in and through each other (Basic Principle 10).

When Ignatius speaks of "finding God in all things," he is talking not merely about finding God's presence and quietly resting in it during prayer time. That famous expression means much more. It also means being with God all day long in our routine duties and activities, doing each thing with God and in God. You are called to be with God and act in God, as God is acting, creating, and giving life in you and all around you. The same is true for each other person. After all, at every moment God is keeping everything in being, from the smallest microbe to the farthest galaxy. God and we are acting and *working side by side* (Stage Three) *and as one* (Stage Four). We are building the Christ together—God in me and I in God. In this way, each of us humans, individually and together, learns to become a "contemplative in action" (Basic Principle 12).

To express this fourth way of loving in prayer, we might say something like:

O Great God in whom I live and act, I no longer wish to live and simply work for you. My deepest desire and the grace I ask is that I may live consciously in you and with you and as a part of your Christ, that I may realize that my primary privilege and honor is to be a cell in the Cosmic Body of Christ. I wish to live and work no longer just as me, but consciously as part of Christ—who holds all of us together on our way to you. For this privilege I offer my deepest thanksgiving.

Conclusion

It is essential not to rush through this contemplation. You may "repeat" this exercise as often as you wish during the preparatory days. You may choose just one point and dwell on it during each "repetition" if you wish. Remember, you will also return to this contemplation at the very end of the Exercises. It is the summation and high point of the Exercises and releases, in time, all the graces you can expect from this process. The richness and graces that flow from this contemplation are inexhaustible.

If you are making the Exercises with others, you may share with each other the insights or special graces you felt during these prayer times. Often, in this kind of sharing, the graces given to you may pass on to others, and the graces of others may flow into you (Basic Principle 10).

It is also important to remember that, while this contemplation engenders in you a deeply personal relationship with the Creator, its ultimate purpose is to help you discover your God-given destiny in the Christ Project and to develop you as a four-level lover of God, others, of our planet, and of all creation (Basic Principle 17).

Note on the Holy Eucharist and Mass

The Eucharist provides the simplest yet most profound synthesis of the *Contemplatio*, since it integrates simultaneously the four stages of that contemplation, namely, Eucharist as (1) gift, (2) side-by-side presence, (3) active working, and (4) mutual indwelling. When the Cosmic Christ who lives today incarnates upon the altar during the celebration of the Mass, there we find God in all things and all things in him.

Therefore, daily Mass and Holy Communion are strongly recommended while making the Exercises as a way to renew the gifts and graces of the *Contemplatio*.

The Principle and Foundation

The Principle and Foundation is a statement of human meaning and purpose emerging from a synthesis of Teilhard's seventeen Basic Principles, which give rise to the New Spiritual Exercises. It assumes we want to be actively involved in and cooperating with what God is doing in the world. The Principle and Foundation takes a most general form and could be accepted by people of any faith. It focuses on what God is trying to accomplish in the world and how humans can help in this co-creative process. It states the core philosophical assertions upon which these new spiritual exercises are based. When accepted as a kind of credo, it becomes the basis of your decisions—major ones as well as everyday ones.

It is not presented as a formal meditation, but as a consideration for your serious reflection. It is meant to be reflected upon sentence by sentence.[1]

PRINCIPLE AND FOUNDATION

You were created to make a unique contribution to the great evolutionary project initiated and continually supported by God, namely, bringing all creation together into one magnificent conscious loving union.

Since all other created things in the universe share with you this common eternal destiny, they are essential to and inseparable from you as you participate in the pursuit of that ongoing evolutionary process.

Individually and joined with others, you are to use all means available to promote and carry out this shared purpose with all your personal creativity, compassion, and energy, always seeking and choosing what is more conducive to that purpose.

For this, God empowers you to grow in passionate love and care for all elements of the cosmos, since they, as you, all live and move and have their being in God's love.

---

1. This Principle and Foundation assumes God has a comprehensive plan or project for all of creation including humanity, and this developing and evolutionary project is really what God is about on Earth. It also assumes we humans, individually and collectively, are meant to be active and proactive co-creators in helping fulfill this plan or project. It is our shared purpose. For Teilhard, as for Saint Paul, this plan or project is expressed as building the Body of the Cosmic Christ.

And God is with you as you undergo whatever diminishments may befall you as you cooperate with others in your efforts and actions in pursuing this divine project—the purpose for which we, individually and collectively, were created.

This Principle and Foundation omits Ignatius' word *indifference*, but not his intent or meaning. Ultimately, Ignatian indifference is about the freedom to meet God and collaborate with God in all circumstances, even if those circumstances are the opposite of what we instinctively want for others and ourselves. This understanding is an integral part of what Teilhard means by the concept of "diminishment."

The Thanksgiving Examen

Throughout his life Teilhard remained an optimist, despite the rejection he suffered from his religious order and from the official church because of his evolutionary ideas. In his prayer, instead of putting his attention on his failures and disappointments, he focused much more on praise, reverence, and gratitude when he related to God.

In recent years, psychologists have discovered a basic law of psychological and spiritual life. We might call it the first law of spiritual energy. It is simply this: *Energy follows attention*. In other words, wherever you focus your attention is where the energy of your body, mind, and spirit goes.

In terms of this first law of spiritual energy, Teilhard preferred to focus, with God's grace, on his own resilience, his capacity to adapt and to restore his enthusiasm for his work and relationships. He was willing to try anything for Christ. If he was blocked from pursuing one avenue, he found another way. He kept his eye on his vision of the evolutionary Christ Project, the work for which he was created. Teilhard realized, as Paul Hawken put it in his book *Blessed Unrest*, "Evolution is optimism in action."

Teilhard's life suggests a nightly review of your day focusing on what went right instead of what went wrong. If you focus on giving and receiving love, your thinking will change for the better. If you focus on thinking good thoughts, your heart will grow more loving. The heart and mind are always interacting in concert.

This process is known as the Thanksgiving Examen (Basic Principle 15). It has five steps.

THE THANKSGIVING EXAMEN

1. To give thanks in general to God our Lord for the benefits received in your life, in others, and in the world today.

2. To ask for grace to recognize all those particular things that happened to you and others that you should personally be grateful for.

3. To take account of your day from the hour that you arose up to the present time, hour by hour, or period by period: first your good thoughts, ideas, and intentions; then your good words spoken and heard; and then good acts,

your actions and those of others, small or large, that positively touched your life or the life of someone else. Record these in your journal.

4. To praise and thank God our Lord for all the opportunities you had to make a difference in the world today and to inspire you to recognize more and more such opportunities in the future.

5. To thank God for all God has done for you, and to ask yourself: What can I envision doing that would lead me to be even more deeply grateful? Close with the Our Father.

Frequency

The Thanksgiving Examen is meant to be a lifelong practice. It may be done at the end of each day, though it can be done more frequently as you feel drawn. Ignatius recommended twice a day, once before the midday meal and once before sleep at night. The more frequently you perform it, the more natural it becomes. And the more grateful you become, the more loving you become, and the more receptive to love you become. In this way, the Examen provides a way of growing into an ever-closer relationship with God and with others.

Eyes on Your Destiny

It is another well-known psychological truth that *success breeds success*. Failure tends to breed anxiety, embarrassment, more focus on failure, and feelings of disappointment. As all good athletes know, it is better to focus on your good points than to dwell upon what you don't do well. In the spiritual life, the same is true. Focus on your strengths, not on your weaknesses or failings. Accentuate the positive. Focus on what is possible, what you can do for Christ (Basic Principle 9).

What is foremost here is achieving your destiny by focusing on your potential. What is the unique personal contribution you can make to the building up of the Body of Christ? No business venture or sporting event is won by stopping to wallow in your mistakes. Success comes from staying in the game, playing your best, and keeping your eye on the goal. In a similar way, God's evolutionary project in Christ will not come about simply by you not committing sin or even by reducing the number of your sins and faults. Observing the rules and not doing what is forbidden in the Ten Commandments is fine, but basically, it produces a holding pattern. It does not promote the true purpose of your life. It deals primarily with "what I should avoid doing for Christ," but misses the more important "what I could be doing for Christ" and "what I want to be doing for Christ."

Ignatius noted that a truly grateful person could never be a sinful person. In fact, in a letter he wrote to fellow Jesuit Simon Rodriguez, he suggested that "ingratitude was likely the cause and source of all evil and sin."[2] One who develops a continual spirit of gratitude by using the Thanksgiving Examen will likely notice many of his or her undesirable faults falling by the wayside. Certainly, by also being grateful for others' good qualities, you come to love others more easily.

---

2. Letter to Simon Rodriguez, March 18, 1542. Ignatius describes ingratitude as "*causa y principio de todos los males y pecados.*"

The Positive Particular Examen

Ignatius' Particular Examen might also be revisited in a positive way, to develop your strengths. Thus, instead of counting the number of times you made critical remarks to others today, count the number of times you found ways to notice the good qualities of others and affirmed them. Or, instead of counting the times you were afraid to speak up, begin counting the times when you did speak up, and thank God each time (Basic Principle 14).

As these more desirable thoughts, words, and deeds increase in frequency, your ability to perform them gets stronger. They grow easier to carry out and feel more natural.

Practicing these positive strengths will allow undesirable behaviors to diminish and disappear. This is because of another very basic law of psychological and spiritual energy, namely, that *what is practiced gets reinforced*. Why? Because *energy follows attention*.

THE POSITIVE PARTICULAR EXAMEN

1. Upon rising, you may take a few moments to remind yourself about the particular good words or deeds you want to develop today and ask God to help you recognize opportunities for practicing this desirable behavior.

2. At the first Thanksgiving Examen of your day, perhaps before lunch, let yourself actually count the times you succeeded in practicing your desirable activity, and thank God for your success. Make a record of these in your journal.

3. At the second Thanksgiving Examen, at bedtime, again count the times you succeeded in practicing your desirable activity, and thank God for your success. If you wish, you can compare this count with your earlier count.

Those who have progressed through the First and Second Weeks of the Exercises may choose to begin making a fuller Thanksgiving Examen. In this approach, you may enumerate not only the things you are most grateful for but also the things you are "not so grateful for."

Notice that you do not describe the things you are not grateful for as "what went wrong" or "where I failed" or "how I have sinned." You are simply *not so grateful* that you feel this way or that this thing happened or that you said or did this or that. There is a big difference in formulating an experience in this way. Where there is gratitude, even just a small amount, God's grace is not blocked.

For example, if you feel discouraged, surround your discouragement with gratitude. For example, "God, thank you for my being conscious of this unwelcome feeling. I know you love me and all that is going on within me at this moment. With each breath I take, I trust that I am receiving whatever grace I need to receive from you. If I cannot change what I am not so grateful for, help me to accept it" (Basic Principle 5).

You may also ask yourself: "What can I learn from this experience?" Or, "What is God trying to teach me from this experience?"

It is important to keep unwelcome experiences or feelings surrounded in gratitude, for gratitude generates positive outcomes: it opens up your mind to new learning and your heart to new grace. It also nurtures growth in consciousness (Basic Principle 3).

Introduction to the Meditations on Sin

Devolution and Sin

Evolutionary spirituality calls upon us to use all our talents and energies to struggle against any form of devolution, any turning back or holding back the progressive development of the universal Body of Christ. The Christ Project is aiming toward the ever-growing consciousness of the human race of its oneness with all creation.

Any conscious turning back to the past or retreating to a safer place for no good reason is *de*volution, not evolution. Of course, there is such a thing as a kind of retreat for the sake of maturation and learning. Again, there are times when a person or group needs to move into a safe place, as in a retreat, to recoup their energy, reconnect to mission, and restrategize. In these cases, the overall intention is not to quit but to move forward and upward, to keep evolving.

In an evolutionary spirituality, which is by its very nature a proactive spirituality, conscious choices to refuse to go forward would be seen as sin or human weakness.

We are invited to keep pressing forward and upward using our attractiveness—our peacefulness, warmth, approachableness, enthusiasm, cooperation, humor, etc.—to initiate and form strong relationships that are willing to work together, with love, to push the envelope. We are invited also to keep using our willingness to embrace complexity and our longing to become more and more conscious to reveal what can be.

What, then, might be considered sinful behavior or thoughts within this divine milieu perspective?

The traditional notion of sin as primarily an offense against God is still true, even in an evolutionary spirituality. It is certainly true today that people are consciously violating the commandments of God in doing what is against love, compassion, forgiveness, and healing. People still lie, steal, cheat, abuse, and kill others to promote their own wealth, power, and pride. They consciously harbor in their hearts jealousy, hatred, revenge, resentment, lust, and greed.

However, it is assumed that people making these New Spiritual Exercises are not consciously and seriously violating the commandments, but are rather on a spiritual path where lying, cheating, stealing, abusing, and killing are not part of their intentions or behavior. In other words, it is assumed that those making these Exercises are not habituated to a sinful way of life, but are rather committed to living a life of love, compassion, forgiveness, and healing (Basic Principles 2 and 3).

The Relationship between Sin and Grace

As you noticed in Basic Principle 15, these Exercises shift the traditional relationship between sin and grace.

In the traditional relationship between sin and grace, it is assumed that the more you consciously reflect on your personal sins and failures, the more you will desire God's generous forgiving and redemptive grace so that you may serve God even more generously. For many people this relationship between sin and grace is powerful.

The relationship between sin and grace suggested by an evolutionary spirituality, one that is creation-centered, is somewhat different. It (1) follows a different dynamic, (2) uses another source of motivation, (3) has a wider definition of sin, and (4) creates a new context for understanding sin and grace.

First, it follows a different dynamic. God's evolutionary proactive love for the Christ Project becomes the foundational experience of God's love for me, since God has made me a unit of the Christ Body. It is God's love for the Christ Project that puts the spotlight on my failure to act accordingly.

Second, it uses another source of motivation. Sin in this evolutionary view focuses primarily on the refusal to strive to live up to one's potential. It begins with the grace to realize that, even though I am not formally violating the commandments, I am nevertheless choosing not to do things in many cases I could easily be doing to build up the Body of Christ. Here, I am motivated to seek the grace to respond generously to God's call to be proactive on behalf of the Christ Project.

Third, it has a wider definition of sin. In this evolutionary viewpoint, the focus of sin is on sins of omission,[3] the failure of the good

3. It is interesting to note that the *Confiteor* (I confess...) of the new translation of the Mass retains the request for forgiveness for sins of omission; however, the juxtaposition of the new language (in italics) emphasizes its seriousness. "I confess...that I have *greatly* sinned...in what I have failed to do, *through my fault, through my fault, through my most grievous fault.*"

person who has opportunities to make a difference in his or her milieu, yet does nothing.

Fourth, it creates a new context for understanding sin and grace. God remains loving and forgiving toward me, despite the fact that I am conscious of what I could be doing for Christ and am not doing it—perhaps because of my human weakness. In light of God's unconditional divine love for the Christ Project, I desire the grace to have more courage to be proactive for Christ.

In either approach to sin, during the meditations on sin and grace the retreatant asks God to reveal what he or she may need to be freed, liberated, loosened, healed, strengthened, and transformed. Coming into this awareness is itself a revelatory grace from God, not just simply the fruit of the retreatant's self-reflection. God's love, experienced in the Exercises' opening days, now acts as the revealing agent, uncovering what in you and your world is ripe for transformation (Basic Principle 7).

Activities and Sin

According to Teilhard, all human experience can be divided into two generic groups, which he calls Activities and Passivities. Activities are what we do by our own effort. Our activities include our choices and intentions as well as our physical behavior. Our passivities are those things we undergo or endure and usually have little choice over.

Sin, since it must be a conscious and free act, can occur only in the realm of activities, specifically activities of diminishment.

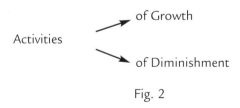

Fig. 2

We can expend our efforts and activities in two ways, either by intending and choosing to do things that promote our growth and development and that of others (Activities of Growth), or by freely intending and choosing to do things that weaken and diminish us and/or others (Activities of Diminishment—see fig. 2).

Activities of diminishment are the activities we perform by free choice that harm others or ourselves. These can be actions that are destructive, harmful, and corrupting, or actions that are traditionally called sinful. Actions that diminish us or other persons are, at the same time, activities that somehow diminish the Body of Christ.

ACTIVITIES I HAVE FAILED TO DO

There is another kind of activity not typically specified among activities of diminishment. These are *activities that are consciously chosen to be left undone.* They might more simply be called "activities of omission."

Specifically for Teilhard, *sin may be found wherever there is the unwillingness to try something for Christ.* Teilhard sees the Christ Project as keeping the cosmic Body of Christ evolving toward its fullest and most complete expression. For him, doing whatever one can to keep the Body of Christ evolving is what we have been put on Earth for. The most obvious sin, for Teilhard, is to know that you are called to promote the Christ Project, yet you consciously refuse to commit yourself to that divine project (Basic Principle 9).

Examples of this might be situations where people see an opportunity to do something that would make a positive difference and may even be eager to do it, but don't follow through because of fear of failure or rejection, anxiety about the negative opinions of others, a lack of self-discipline, insecurity about their abilities, etc. Alternatively, they may let themselves be lured away from the opportunity by some attractive and pleasurable diversion. In other words, sin is knowing there is something you can do—the opportunity is there—to further the development of yourself, other people, or Earth, and you freely choose not to do it, or don't at least try.

Remember that consciousness is defined as *awareness plus appropriate response.* Appropriate activities for you to promote and develop the Christ Project will depend, of course, on your personal situation, your time, your talents, your health, your family obligations, and your financial situation. Again, while refusing to do any of these things would not be seen as formally sinful in a traditional sense, they could be seen so by someone committed to building the Body of Christ (Basic Principle 3).

THE DESTRUCTIVE POWER OF SILENCE OR DOING NOTHING

We don't usually think of human destructive events in history as being shaped by silence, but they are. We don't usually think of sin or evil as *inactivity*, for example, not doing anything or just standing by to see what happens. Yet, as the English philosopher Edmund Burke wisely observed, "The only thing necessary for the triumph of evil is for good men to do nothing."

The key word in that quotation is *only*. Silence and inactivity provide the necessary and sufficient conditions for *de*volution, for a downward descent. For example, some of the "do-nothing" kinds of people include the cynic, the blamer, the bystander, or those who play the victim.

It is not easy to press on beyond the status quo when others resist or try to subvert your effort. It is often a struggle to push against the inertia produced by the fear and laziness around you and in you, the apathy that seeks only comfort and pleasure and does not want to be bothered. Nevertheless, in an evolutionary spirituality, probably some of the worst sins are sins of omission—failures to act when action is called for.

Sins of Omission

The parable of the talents (Matt 25:14–30) is an attempt of Jesus to explain or describe a major dynamic in what we are calling the Christ Project. To be fully effective, both the kingdom of God and the Christ Project need our positive human cooperative response. God is counting on us (Basic Principle 11).

In this parable, the master (God or Christ) expects his servants to be not only active, but also proactive, in promoting and developing the wealth of the master. Each servant is given an amount to work with in terms of their abilities.

Perhaps the most contrasting focus of this passage about the nature of God's relationship to us is on the difference between (1) those who use their talents to make a difference in the world and (2) those who hide their talents and never use them.

Other Unproductive Responses

The parable offers only two categories of response, those who multiply the master's money, and those who do nothing with it. However, when we consider talents not simply as money but in the metaphorical sense as human gifts, skills, and abilities, we observe a much wider range of unproductive responses. These include: people who are totally unconscious of their gifts and talents; others who may know of their talents but don't see their usefulness; those who refuse to exercise their talents because they are not outstanding; those who do not put any value on their talents or appreciate them; and those who are afraid to use their talents in public for fear of embarrassment, failure, shame, disappointment, ridicule, or rejection (Matt 25:14–30).

An Unnoticed Kind of Sin

A very common kind of sin but one that often goes unnoticed—the sin of omission—is at the heart of this parable. Even the servant who hid the money while his master was away did not commit sin in the formal, active sense of the word. He had no intention of stealing his master's money, squandering it, or using it to pay off personal debts. He just kept it safe, but unused. In Christ-Project language, we would say he failed *to make his unique contribution to the great evolutionary project* (Basic Principle 9).

A Practical Challenge

The great task of bringing the Christ Project to its completion involves learning how to use our talents, knowledge, resources, personal connections, and opportunities to further develop and deepen the consciousness of the whole world. Everything you do—*or don't do*—affects the Body of Christ (Basic Principle 12).

As Saint Paul says in First Corinthians, the Holy Spirit has given a variety of gifts to different members of the community, but these gifts are all given for the building up of the Body of Christ. Everyone has a unique set of gifts, talents, and opportunities (see 1 Cor 12:1–31). You may be healthy and active, or sickly and weak. You may be outgoing or reserved, vivacious or dull, handsome or common, tall or short, slender or chubby, beautiful or ordinary. You may be rich or poor. You may come from a loving family or an abusive one. You may be lonely, sick, rejected, physically or mentally handicapped, or even in prison. The task is for you to discover the gifts you have and find creative ways to use them in your community and situation.

EVEN GREATER RESPONSIBILITY

One might think that the servants who had doubled their money would have received an immediate heavenly reward so that they could retire and relax for the rest of their days. Instead, the master gave them even greater responsibilities in their earthly life. If the master considered responsibility for ten million dollars (ten talents in today's money) something small (Matt 25:23), imagine what those "greater responsibilities" might involve!

Jesus reinforces this notion of God's project when he says, "From everyone to whom much has been given, much will be required; and from one to whom much has been entrusted, even more will be demanded" (Luke 12:48).

Parable of the Talents: Meditation on Sins of Omission (Basic Principle 9; Matthew 25:14–30)

First Prelude: Take some moments to realize that each person being born has certain talents, graces, gifts, resources, and opportunities. Each one is being enabled in his or her own unique ways to help develop and build the Body of Christ on Earth.

Second Prelude: Imagine Jesus trying to find an image or story to convey some meaning of God's ways to his listeners and to the grand project God has in mind for them, especially about being able to co-create with him. Then, picture him telling this story of the talents.

Third Prelude: You may ask for the grace of generosity and industriousness in working at the Christ Project. You may also ask to be more proactive like the first two servants. You may also pray to become aware of how you may be hiding or not using your talents.

1. What the First Two Servants Are Doing. Here you may use your imagination to see what each of these servants does with the money entrusted to them (Think of a talent as equivalent to one million dollars today), how they invest these talents in different ways, how they perhaps encourage each other and share ideas. Since all three of them probably continue to live together in the master's house, they have many opportunities to talk to each other and support each other. After you talk with them, ask them to point out what talents you have been given by God and how you might use them to further the Christ Project (Basic Principle 10).

2. What the Third Servant Is Doing and Not Doing. Here you may use your imagination to probe the mind of the third servant. Ask him why he does not imitate his fellow servants in their creative and productive investing, why he chose simply to hide his master's money, and how he responds to the other two servants as they talk about how they are multiplying what they have been given. Ask him what kinds of feelings are going through him all the while—fear, anger, resentment, annoyance, relief, or some other emotions.

3. Why Is the Master So Disappointed with the Third Servant? Here you may talk to the master and ask him what evokes such strong reaction to the third servant. You may ask the master, if you were to be one of the three servants reporting to him today, what kind of a reaction he would have to you.

Colloquy: Here it will be to talk to the Creator, Christ, or Mary about your response to three questions:

What have I done to help build the Body of Christ?
What am I doing to help build the Body of Christ?
What am I going to do to help build the Body of Christ?

You may tell them of your sorrow at having omitted things, actions that would have been simple and easy to do, as well as some more challenging things that would have required effort and courage to accomplish. You may ask for grace to be more sensitive to opportunities that present themselves from now on.

Review: As a very practical response to this meditation, *make a list of your various resources, talents, and abilities* (Basic Principle 6). You should be able to list at least twenty or thirty. Remember, it is not important that your abilities be of the highest order. For example, you may not be a gourmet chef, but you may be an adequate cook, well-organized, enthusiastic, a good helper in the kitchen, a good shopper, a very appreciative diner, and a fine dish-dryer, etc. All of these abilities in their own little ways can help build loving connections in the Body of Christ. As you add each new item to your list, say a word of thanks for being able to use that ability to build the Body of Christ.

Use your Particular Examen to help develop or practice some skill or ability useful for the Christ Project.

Introduction to Social Sin

We Are All One

Whether we like it or not, all human beings on Earth are inextricably linked together in many ways—genetically, biologically, psychologically, socially, politically, economically, electronically, and in a larger evolutionary process. As one person put it, "Each of us is a vital thread in every other person's tapestry. Our lives are woven together for a reason. So, the next time you hear someone is facing a problem and you think it doesn't concern you...." Humans are essentially social beings, continually interdependent on others from conception to death (Basic Principle 16).

That we are each a unique being is also true; I am I and you are you. That we are separable beings is false; I cannot live independently or separate from you, from other human beings, or from nature. Just as we each can sin personally, it is also true that we can sin as a society. Social sin and personal sin are mutually reinforcing. Though inseparable in fact, they can be distinguished in theory.

Social sin is systemic, that is, it is manifested and "lives" in the social structures functioning in the larger society. Jesus spent much of his public ministry stirring up awareness of some of the most hurtful social evils of his day, like religious hypocrisy among the priests and Pharisees, corrupt systems of justice perpetuated by the lawyers and scribes, unfair treatment of the poor by the rich, biased treatment of women, the social ostracism of tax collectors and the ritually impure, etc. Truly, Jesus bore the damaging effects of these social sins because he felt their evil impact daily on his own body and soul and on those around him (Basic Principle 4).

He had not contributed to these social sins or tolerated them, as we have. He was like us in all things but sin. Yet these evils were laid on him. They diminished him and his ability to convert people to a change of heart. What diminished him and the people were not only the personal sins of Caiaphas, Pilate, or Judas, but also, perhaps even more powerfully, the social evils of humanity.

These, and other unjust structures more prevalent today—militarism, a culture of violence and fear, unfair labor practices, slavery, racism, drug addiction, alcoholism, political graft, materialism, individualism, and many more—are subtle but all-pervasive social and cultural patterns, larger than any individual or group, that lead or tempt us toward injustice and away from mutual love and respect. We have all contributed to these destructive forces, and we have all—all those who ever lived—suffered under them (Basic Principle 1).

An Anti-Evolutionary System

Social sin and personal sin mutually reinforce each other in an interactive anti-evolutionary way. For example, these devolutionary social, cultural, political, and economic arrangements (social sins) distort our personal perceptions of reality. They often restrain our abilities to such an extent that we, individually and collectively, find it harder to choose what is good and easier to choose evil. For example, at work people find it increasingly easy to expend minimal effort on the job or to cheat and lie to get ahead. At school, students might say, "Why not cheat on exams, be sexually promiscuous, or get drunk, since everybody is doing it?"

Social sin emerges from within this immense living system that we call the cosmic Body of Christ. Using the metaphor of an infection or poison, social sin is toxic to the health of the Body of Christ and hinders its development. Its destructiveness is a systemic reality, a product of countless interactions among humans and nature for centuries, passed on from generation to generation.

Beginning in early childhood and continuing throughout life, we learn almost everything that we know and do by imitating the behaviors and values of those who surround us. Without realizing it, we learn from others both how to bless *and* curse, both how to be good *and* bad, both how to be caring *and* selfish, both how to be generous *and* greedy, both how to be humble *and* proud, both how to cooperate *and* dominate, both how to work hard *and* be lazy, both how to praise *and* humiliate (Basic Principle 6).

A Network of Powers
Creating an Unjust System

Theologian Walter Wink has described a worldwide network of "unjust economic relations, oppressive political relations, biased race relations, patriarchal gender relations, hierarchical power relations, and the use of violence to maintain them all."[4] He has named it the "domination system." Jesus and his contemporaries experienced an unjust system like this under the domination of Rome. Today, we experience it just as strongly under various forms of domination. This basic oppressive structure has persisted for at least five thousand years. Wink writes:

> Those in power created or evolved new myths to socialize women, the poor, and captives into their now-inferior status. Priesthoods, backed up by armies, courts of law, and executioners, inculcated in people's minds the fear of terrible, remote, and inscrutable deities. Wife-beating and child-beating began to be seen as not only normal but a male right. Evil was blamed on women.[5]

In every culture, Wink observes, the domination system took over. "Human destiny was driven in a direction that few would have consciously chosen." Violence became the language of dominance and the major tool of the domination system. Thus, people came to believe false truths: that violence is what will save us, that war produces peace, and that might makes right. In short, the domination system presents violence as redemptive.

Today, violence is so prevalent that it has even become the primary source of entertainment, from children's cartoons to adolescent comic books, from computer games to professional sports, from the almost orgiastic scenes of violence in today's films to gratuitous expressions of violence portrayed in the vast majority of so-called law-enforcement shows on television.

All these human organizations—entertainment, sports, religion, politics, industries, and the rest—that help perpetuate the domination system and the myth of redemptive violence need to be called back to their divine vocations. They need to come to the realization that love, not violence, will ultimately save us; that war produces only more war; that might is meant to serve, not dominate (Basic Principle 9).

---

4. Walter Wink, *The Powers That Be: Theology for a New Millennium* (New York: Doubleday, 1998), 39.

5. Ibid., 41.

Social sin constitutes the primary human condition that cries out for transcendence and grace. If social structures can be sin-full, then they also have the potential to become grace-full, imbued with the power of the Holy Spirit (Basic Principle 15).

Teilhard de Chardin once hopefully asked, "Are there unknown inner resources within the human species that, if brought to the surface, might make it possible for us not only to survive, but also grow beyond our destructive tendencies?" His answer was a hopeful yes. He believed that the power of love could overcome the love of power.

Sadly, however, unjust social structures continue to survive despite the presence of good people—who do nothing. Therefore, not only is an awareness of social structures required, but also a concerted effort is needed to replace unjust structures with ones that promote the betterment of society.

For Jesus, conversion of the heart (*metanoia*) also gives birth to a social conscience. This, in particular, means consciously targeting, through advocacy and by other means, those who are more immediately responsible for perpetuating unjust social structures.

Today, perhaps the best we can do immediately is resist, as Jesus did, in those few areas where we recognize injustice and can do something about it. We can also choose to become agents of change for organizations that try to address and improve certain obvious injustices. The challenge always is to turn a structure that is currently devolutionary into one that is evolutionary, one that is more fitting for the development of the Body of Christ (Basic Principle 3).

Social Responsibility

Changing unjust social structures is a social responsibility. You and I are not individually or personally responsible for social sin in the sense that you or I as individuals could, in a day or a month, change an evil social situation into a just and merciful one. Even Jesus couldn't do that. The fact is that we are involved in these social sins; we participate in them, no matter how hard we may try to avoid them.

It is the responsibility of society as a society to make the needed changes. In other words, the responsibility for making the change is primarily a social responsibility, not an individual one. With respect to a certain social sin, such as racism or abuse, society as a whole can choose through its laws and values to act responsibly or irresponsibly.

Nevertheless, even though changing evil social structures is the responsibility of society, individual attitudes and behavior can have an impact on changing destructive social patterns (Basic Principle 11).

Social Sin and the Crucifixion

Because social sins and personal sins are tied together so inextricably, it is inadequate to say that in his crucifixion Christ died only for our personal sins. What is much more realistic is that Jesus of Nazareth very consciously died bearing the weight of the social sins of organized society, those very sins he openly struggled to confront during his ministry. We might call them, collectively, the sins of humanity. Of course, our personal sins are bound up in those social evils and have contributed to their continued existence.

During his lifetime, Jesus found it very easy to declare "forgiven" the sins of individual people. The gospel writings are full of such stories. What he kept facing head on, and what gave him the most resistance, were those ingrained destructive patterns of society. He bore them throughout his life and they brought him to the cross. He bore them to his death in the direct experience of their power. On the cross, he came into collision with the totality of social evil and social sin.

His solidarity with the human race reveals a primary reason for his death. He died on the cross, in obedience to his gospel and in his solidarity with a selfish humanity that was bent on diminishing itself. His death is his triumphal act asserting that love, not selfishness, is the true basis for human society. Love is the life force of the Body of Christ.

Social Sin: Meditation (Basic Principle 16)

First Prelude: Imagine you are somewhere above Earth, perhaps in a spaceship, looking down and seeing the network of sinful social structures keeping people from living full human lives and hindering the development of the Christ Project. You can see dominator people trying publicly to deny the harm these evil structures are doing to the human race and to nature itself. You can see others observing the destruction, yet doing nothing, or perhaps looking for someone to blame in order to absolve themselves. Still others, perhaps, feel helpless or too cowardly to say or do anything to make a difference. Others are resisting one specific social evil but without a true change of heart, and so end up, perhaps unwittingly, supporting different social evils: for example, some may condemn abortion, yet support the death penalty.

Second Prelude: Join Jesus and his companions as they confront the social sins that burden the people around them.

Third Prelude: Ask for the grace to see the pervasive power of social sin and how I personally, if unconsciously, reinforce it. Ask for the grace to resist it and, with a change of heart, the grace to make a fundamental choice to transform society in those little or large ways I can. Ask for the grace to find others who share my commitment to making a positive difference in a certain area of concern. Ask for the grace to see the immense divine forgiveness flowing upon the human race that liberates me and stretches my heart to be ready to respond to God's call.

1. Consider Jesus confronting the Pharisees about their religious hypocrisy, and the lawyers about the unnecessary burdens they place on ordinary people without lifting a finger to ease these burdens (see Luke 11:37–54). The Pharisees and lawyers are so unconsciously habituated to the social diminishment they help perpetuate that they cannot see it as a personal or social sin.

2. Consider Jesus confronting the moneychangers in the temple in their greed and obsession with making a profit (see Luke 19:45–46; also Luke 16:9–13). The startled moneychangers are so used to performing their generations-old function that they may have convinced themselves they are performing a ministry, not perpetuating a social injustice. Talk to them—and to Jesus—about it.

3. Consider Jesus confronting the mistreatment of women: in their capacity for love and generosity (see Luke 7:36–50 and Luke 21:1–4); in their capacity to think as well as men (see John 4:1–26 and Luke 10:38–42); against men's violent treatment of them (see John 8:1–11); in the financial abuse

of women (see Luke 8:43–48 and Luke 7:11–17). The Jewish men took offense, claiming that even in the Ten Commandments God seems to imply that women and wives are the possessions of men, much as their homes, land, and cattle are their possessions.

Colloquy: Perhaps you can speak to Jesus on the cross. See how he bears the weight of the social sins of organized society, those very sins he openly struggled to confront during his ministry, those sins you and I continue to support by our choices and our inactivity.

You may acknowledge the inescapability of social sin—how it is almost impossible to avoid participating in it—and how the only possible hope in the situation is God's mercy, forgiveness, and transforming grace. In this context, divine forgiveness given visibly on the cross remains an essential expression of God's love and grace given to us. This forgiveness liberates us and renews us to be able to work confidently for Christ and God's divine project.

Sin and the Christ Project: Meditation (Basic Principle 9)

First Prelude: Take some moments to reflect on how important the Christ Project is to the Creator, the Word, and the Holy Spirit, and some of the countless ways individuals and groups easily could participate actively in the Christ Project.

Second Prelude: Recognize the tremendous potential across the planet for advancing the Christ Project in every area of life and endeavor, or imagine how far advanced the Christ Project could be if everyone was already doing what they could to further its development and successful outcome.

Third Prelude: Here, ask for the grace to realize that, even though I am not formally violating the commandments, I am nevertheless *not* doing as much as I could be doing to build up the Body of Christ. Ask also for the grace to respond to God's invitation to be generously and courageously proactive for Christ. You may also ask for the grace to recognize new ways or opportunities to respond to God's invitation to participate in the great Christ Project.

1. *What Others Are Already Doing.* Reflect on the Holy Spirit inspiring many people around the world to carry out tasks, individually and in groups, that would bring about more love, compassion, healing, and forgiveness on Earth. Think of other groups helping to make advances in biology, chemistry, genetics, medicine, surgery, pharmacology, agriculture, fuel efficiency, alternative energies, technology, communication, pure research, space exploration, undersea exploration, ecology, and so on. Give thanks for the Holy Spirit's inspirations and blessing for all these undertakings that are helping the Christ Project.

2. *What You Are Doing.* Saint Ignatius suggests that you reflect on the three questions below. He also suggests that you imagine doing your reflections at the foot of the cross looking at Jesus crucified. This face-to-face confrontation is meant to generate a deeply personal realization of Jesus' act as an expression of God's evolutionary proactive love. It provides a foundational experience for you of God's love.

- *What have I done for Christ?* Here, perhaps with pen and paper, you might list things in the past that you have already done to develop your own talents, skills, wisdom, and consciousness, and what you have already done to make a positive difference in the world.
- *What am I doing for Christ?* Here you might list things you are currently doing to keep developing your body, mind, and spirit, as well as what you are doing to better the planet within your sphere of influence.
- *What could I do for Christ?* Here you might list some of the things you hope to accomplish for Christ that involve your own betterment as well as the world in general.

3. *What You Are Not Doing.* Take each of the three questions above and note what you have omitted doing. Again carry out your reflections at the foot of the cross looking at Jesus crucified. In the back of your mind is the Christ Project, God's plan to unify all creation in the Cosmic Christ.

Asking these questions in the context of the cross will show that it is God's love, not God's anger that reveals—that shines the light on—our sin.

- *What have I not done for Christ?* Here, you might list some of the times in the past that you have had the opportunity to make a positive difference in terms of your own talents, skills, wisdom, and consciousness, and the opportunities you had, but didn't.
- *What am I now not doing for Christ?* Here, you might list some of the things you are not currently doing that you could be doing to keep developing your body, mind, and spirit, as well as helping better the planet.
- *What could I do for Christ that currently I have no plans to do?* Here, you might list some of the things you may soon have the opportunity to accomplish for your own betterment as well as for others and the world in general, opportunities you have yet no plans to take advantage of.

Colloquy: In the presence of Jesus on the Cross, feel his infinite love for you as you review what you have written in your lists. Let your heart speak to him. Express your sorrow at having shortchanged what you could have been doing for him and with him in the Christ Project. Ask for the grace to overcome any fear or lack of faith and courage that may be keeping you from doing all you can for Christ. Ask for the grace to realize that, despite what you have not done, you are still a full and respected member of God's family.

End of the First Week

Journal Review

Before you begin the Second Week of the Exercises, it is important to gather and reflect upon the graces and insights of the First Week. One of the best ways of doing this is to reflectively reread all the entries in your retreat journal, starting from the beginning.

Set aside at least an hour for this grace-filled process.

Begin with a prayer for guidance, asking that in the rereading of your journal you may not miss any insight or grace you received, especially in relation to your purpose in making the Exercises.

As you reread your journal entries, things may strike you that you may not have noticed before now. Underline them.

As you notice each grace or insight, say a simple thank you to God.

On a fresh page of your journal, write "First Week Journal Review" and begin listing on this page the insights and graces of the First Week that you especially want to remember.

Close the process with a colloquy of gratitude, perhaps one with Our Lady, another with Christ, and one with the Creator.

Note: If you are making the Exercises in a small group or team, it may be useful to share with your team members some of what you have written on your First Week journal review pages.

The Second Week

The Call of the Kingdom

A Radical Mind Shift

What Ignatius is primarily trying to do in his kingdom meditation—and many miss this point—is to foster a major mental shift in the retreatant's mind. The shift calls for a fundamental choice that would likely change the focus of most people's lives and life purpose. However, for you the shift is necessary in order to enter into a proper mind-set for the Second Week of the Exercises.

The shift calls you from seeing your spiritual purpose as simply seeking individual salvation, which is probably the life purpose of most believers, to committing your life to help carry out a divine project on Earth. In the original kingdom meditation, Ignatius has Christ refer to the divine project as "this work" (96). When you make the fundamental choice to pursue this divine work, your primary expenditure of energy and attention shifts from striving for personal salvation to involvement in the divine project. Ignatius invites retreatants to begin thinking on a global scale: *accepting responsibility for helping the Holy Spirit "renew the face of Earth"* (Basic Principle 9).

The Divine Project

Christ's project, as we read in Ignatius' kingdom text, involves nothing less than transforming the "whole world" (95). It will certainly call for hard work ("share the labor with me"), and will require great generosity of service ("They will make offerings of greater worth and moment.") (97). In this meditation, Jesus is inviting us to join him in a special project, initiated by God, which is so important that it needed God's own Son to reveal it clearly and accurately—and to spearhead it.

Ignatius wants you to feel the excitement of this call. It requires a conversion of heart because Jesus is calling you to love all people and to accept responsibility for everyone, rather than limiting that responsibility merely to your own life and immediate family. See, for example, Romans 14:7, 20–23 and Matthew 25:34–40.

In the light of this divine project, each of us has a destiny, a part that we alone can fulfill. Christ calls each one who can hear the call to that unique destiny and contribution to the divine project. Jesus is putting his trust in you and me.

Love Is Central

Jesus reveals that the nature of God is unconditional love and that this divine love is creative, active, and plan-centered; it is also forward looking, proactive, and evolutionary. God has nurtured a loving plan for creation since the beginning. The plan was announced to us by Christ. We may be *invited* or called to join the ranks of the generous ones who follow Jesus but, once we join, we are *commanded* to love one another (John 13:34). Nothing less than unconditional love for all humans and all of creation—learning to love the way God loves, as you experienced it in the first contemplation—will suffice for workers participating in this divine project. This love that Jesus and Ignatius are talking about is no emotional infatuation or attachment. It is a mature love that thrives on a shared responsibility to carry out a project— "that they may be one as you, Father, and I are one" (John 17:20–23). To accomplish this, each individual is called to become God's co-worker (*synergos* in Greek, see 1 Cor 3:8–9, 21–23).

Ignatius is talking about covering the planet with people exuding unconditional love. It is only love that will conquer all. It is probably appropriate to say that, ultimately, Ignatius' kingdom meditation is really a parable about *the power and attraction of real love on the human heart*, more than about kings and knights. To learn to love God passionately we must also learn to love the cosmos passionately—and to love passionately its potential, its "not yet."

A New Perspective on the Kingdom Meditation

While some describe the grace for this meditation as to "fall in love with Jesus," Teilhard would have you also ask for the grace to fall in love with the cosmos (Basic Principle 12). While Ignatius focuses on Christ of the Gospels, Teilhard's focus is also on the Christ of the Cosmos. Teilhard introduces us to an evolutionary way of understanding the kingdom meditation (Basic Principle 17).

Perhaps a quotation from the flyleaf of a recent book may best describe an appropriate perspective for an evolutionary kingdom meditation that we need for a new century.

> The dawn of the twenty-first century has witnessed two remarkable developments in our history: the appearance of systemic problems that are genuinely global in scope, and the growth of a worldwide movement that is determined to heal the wounds of the earth with the force of passion, dedication, and collective intelligence and wisdom. Across the planet groups ranging from ad-hoc neighborhood associations to well-funded international organizations are confronting issues like the destruction of the environment, the abuses of free-market fundamentalism, social justice, and the loss of indigenous cultures. They share no orthodoxy or unifying ideology; they follow no single charismatic leader; they remain supple enough to coalesce easily into larger networks to achieve their goals. While they are mostly unrecognized by politicians and the media, they are bringing about what may one day be judged the single most profound transformation of human society.[1]

According to Paul Hawken, there are at least two million organizations worldwide—people with good hearts—working toward ecological sustainability and issues related to social justice. These separate organizations form a global, leaderless conglomerate that reaches every corner of the world. Hawken says this movement is "dispersed, inchoate, and fiercely independent. It has no shared manifesto or common doctrine, no overriding authority to check with" (p. 3). It is taking place in schoolrooms, farms, jungles, villages, companies, deserts, fisheries, slums, and even in hotel rooms.

From an evolutionary perspective, this movement is, without a doubt, the most complex association of human beings ever assem-

---

1. Paul Hawken, *Blessed Unrest: How the Largest Movement in the World Came into Being and Why No One Saw It Coming* (New York: Penguin, 2007).

bled. Most people know only the organizations they happen to be linked with. But its global database is mammoth. It is also facing issues that governments often fail to tackle: energy, jobs, conservation, poverty, and global warming. How it appears to function as a coherent system is even more mysterious (Basic Principle 8).

Compelling, coherent, innovative, organic, self-organized congregations involving tens of millions of people are dedicated to change. "What I see," says Hawken, "are ordinary and some not-so-ordinary individuals willing to confront despair, power, and incalculable odds in an attempt to restore some semblance of grace, justice, and beauty to this world" (p. 4).

For those who have eyes to see, collectively, this unnamed movement, this healing life force striving for social justice and planetary concern under and through and around national boundaries, is the Spirit at work in the Christ Project. It is a conspiracy of love. All of these small and large groups are intertwining, creating a complex web of creative and compassionate relationships connecting the whole world, each one in its own way helping create conditions that are more conducive to life. People in each group probably love someone or something that is suffering or needs support; they are moved by compassion and concern. They do not want to see people suffer. They do not want to leave a broken world to their children and grandchildren. To begin to find your place—if you have not already found it—you have only to use an Internet search engine to find the issue or the concern where you'd like to connect (Basic Principle 7).

The Kingdom: Meditation (Basic Principle 9)

First Prelude: Picture the universe as one single immense entity beloved of God and living in a graced milieu of God's love.

Second Prelude: Direct your focus to Earth and picture all of humanity living and moving and interacting in this great Body of Christ as in a divine milieu.

Third Prelude: You may ask for the grace to fall in love with this cosmic-sized Christ that includes all of humanity and the rest of creation, and the desire to be part of bringing the cosmic Body of Christ to its highest potential.

Part One: Ten Thousand Earthly Leaders

1. In the first part of the kingdom meditation—instead of a single earthly king—Teilhard might ask us to imagine ten thousand leaders, men and women, spread all over the cities and villages of the Earth, people of all races and classes, of all religions and no religion, young and old, rich and poor, in storefronts and boardrooms, in homes and churches, in classrooms and picket lines, in jungles and around campfires, in laboratories and offices, who represent ten thousand different caring groups, all rising above their daily difficulties, finding ten thousand different ways to improve Earth and the beings on it. These proactive groups are committed to bringing human rights to all, each in their own way. Some represent community action groups confronting local injustice; others are multinational, seeking solutions to world hunger and poverty; others are research scientists dedicated to finding new drugs to alleviate suffering; some represent authors and journalists who want to write about solutions to local and world problems; some are concerned with literacy and education; some are helping with employment and unemployment; some are working in various branches of ecology; some are philosophers and theologians; some are teachers; some are politicians truly committed to serving the people; some are concerned parents; some have dedicated their lives to devoutly meditating and praying for world peace and cooperation, for an end to war and terrorism. Every possible field or life path you can imagine is represented in this group of leaders.

2. Imagine that as you are standing in this crowd, not knowing where to turn or to whom to speak, one or two of these leaders approach you. You discover they are persons just like you, working in the same area of interest as you, full of compassion and care. They describe to you the ways they are creatively working to improve the conditions of life in their circle of influence. You feel their excitement and enthusiasm. It is contagious. They may even suggest ways that you could uniquely help their group or association

pursue its purpose. Other leaders are approaching other persons like you, who have found their way here.

This group of leaders would be encouraging people to grow beyond their egocentric mind-set and commit themselves to fully developing a geocentric and cosmic mind-set.

Part Two: The Universal Christ (Basic Principle 17)

1. While you imagine yourself still standing amid this crowd of these ten thousand leaders, you can imagine Christ speaking to you, perhaps as a voice heard in your heart, saying:

You see all these people representing thousands of small-to-large organizations worldwide, each with its own compassionate agenda doing its own small part to transform the world. They and all their groups live and move and have their being in me. These groups were meant to come into being and work in peaceful and loving concern for the betterment of all. Each small and large group has been part of the Creator's plan and vision from the beginning of time. That vision is to bring all creation together in one supreme loving union. These people love Earth and all of creation. I invite you to find the individuals and groups to which you are most attracted and most qualified to help, and offer yourself in supporting them. For we all have a long evolutionary way to go to fulfill the Creator's plan. When you hear these leaders speaking to you, realize that it is I speaking to you. When you work with them, realize that it is I working with you, alongside you, within you.

2. Those who want to be more devoted and signalize themselves in service of the Body of Christ, will not only offer their persons to the labor required for the Creator's project, but will also make offerings of greater value and greater importance, saying something like:

Eternal Creator of all things, I want to make my offering with your favor and help, in the presence of your divine Son and in the presence of our compassionate Mother and of all the saints of heaven. I want and desire, and consciously choose, with all my heart, mind, soul, and strength, to be an instrument of God's love and healing in the world. I thank you for the energy and clarity you constantly give, so that I may contribute in those ways I can—whatever the cost—to building up the universal Body of your divine Son on Earth as long as I live.

Note: In a similar way, in the original Spiritual Exercises, Ignatius offers his version of an appropriate colloquy at the end of the call of the kingdom as a suggestion. The colloquy is always something that must come from the heart. Therefore, you can only make the offering that is in your heart if it is to be genuine.

While in his suggested colloquy Ignatius suggests that the retreatant ask for "injury, affronts, and poverty," Teilhard assures us that there will be plenty of unwanted "diminishments" to endure, if one truly and freely chooses with energy and clarity, at whatever the cost, in his or her profession to further the divine project of building the Body of Christ on Earth.[2]

Summary

The job of achieving world peace and justice in today's world is too big for any one person or organization. It is the work of thousands of organizations and individuals worldwide, rich and poor, cooperating in achieving a world at peace and one where the environment, our milieu, is made safe for life to continue.

It is noteworthy that Ignatius does not identify the kingdom with the Roman Catholic Church, but sees Christ's reign as much more expansive, including all people and the entire world. Teilhard might say that the Holy Spirit inspires every human being with the desire to promote the loving unity of all beings, except that many are not yet conscious of that inner desire; and among those who are con-

---

2. See section 2 of Teilhard's *The Divine Milieu*, "The Divinization of Our Passivities" (New York: Harper & Row, 1962, 1968).

scious of it, many have not yet said a committed yes to it. Evoking that committed yes is the purpose of Ignatius' kingdom meditation.

Teilhard offers us a fuller picture of the "work" of God's reign, namely, completing the Christ Project. The broad scope of this divine project offers people in every walk of life concrete ways to proactively cooperate in the evolving divine plan. He shows how the global humanitarian movements arising from the bottom up are organically inspired by the grace flowing throughout the divine milieu. These people and groups represent an instinctive collective response of the human spirit, inspired by God, to many different needs and challenges around the planet. What these people and groups are in effect telling us, perhaps still unconscious of what they are saying, is that the Body of Christ is alive and well in our day.

The Call of Jesus

Purpose

A dialogue prayer may be used following the kingdom meditation as a reinforcement of it. It may also help you see how you have been called by God many times in your life, perhaps even in your youth.

Jesus' Early Divine Calling

We are used to thinking that Jesus was first called to ministry after he came to be baptized in the Jordan by his cousin John. However, Jesus' call from God came much earlier. According to Luke's narrative, the first time Jesus heard the divine call was when he came to the temple in Jerusalem at the age of twelve (Luke 2:41–52). As with all of the stories of Jesus' childhood, we have no evidence they actually happened as Luke or Matthew relates them. However, each story reveals an important theological point.

Luke provides an unusual context to make his point. The holy family has been in Jerusalem celebrating a special Passover, because Jesus, at age twelve, most likely has recently been confirmed in his Jewish manhood with his bar mitzvah. When the group from Nazareth begins to return home, Jesus goes against his parents' expectations and remains behind in Jerusalem. When they discover he is missing, they retrace their steps to the Holy City to find him debating in the temple with the teachers and amazing them with his wisdom. When his parents confront him with his apparent disobedience, he gives them an enigmatic reply, which scripture scholars have struggled for many centuries to translate meaningfully.

The traditional translation of Jesus' reply to his parents is "Why were you looking for me? Did you not know that I must be about my Father's business?" The Jerusalem Bible translates it, "Why were you looking for me? Did you not know that I must be busy with my Father's affairs?" The New Revised Standard Version says, "Why were you searching for me? Did you not know that I must be in my Father's house?" Even scripture scholars acknowledge that none of these translations is satisfying.

At one time, I was in Nazareth and our guide, who spoke Aramaic, the familiar language of Jesus and the apostles, told me that all the English translations of this passage had missed the point. He explained to me that among Aramaic-speaking people in Palestine, the idiomatic phrase that the young Jesus used in responding to his parents had much more the meaning, *"I heard my Father call my name, and how could I not respond?"*

The Holy Land guide's translation showed that Jesus' reply to his parents was announcing three things: (1) the fact that, during that Passover time, Jesus had received his divine calling; (2) that he knows who his true Father is; and (3) that he has responded to his Father's call.

Jesus was not simply a rebellious teenager defying the expectations of his parents by staying behind in Jerusalem, nor was he a child prodigy in theology who loved to show off in front of the teachers. He was a young person who had heard unmistakably an overpowering divine call.

He had said "yes" to that call, just as his mother had said "yes" to the divine call in her youth, and just as Joseph had said "yes" to the call he had received in a dream. His parents, Luke tells us, did not understand the meaning or importance of what Jesus was saying to them. But we do.

Whether Luke's story in its details is factual is irrelevant. His point is that Jesus heard a divine call and said "yes" to it.

The point of this meditation is that, like Jesus, Mary, and Joseph, we all—each of us individually—receive a divine call, or perhaps more than one, to help complete the Body of Christ on Earth.

Your Divine Call

Many people will say they have not heard anything like a divine call nor would they know how to recognize it. The playwright Eugene O'Neill once said, "Most of us die with our own music still inside us." It is as though God has invited us to sing, and many do not know what to sing or how to sing. They do not even know they have their own music inside them. Or, if they do, they do not know how to let it out. They die without knowing they can make a difference.

Here are some simple ways to help you identify God's call. Your calling—the kind of work you were meant to do to foster the divine plan—may often be found in any or all of the following situations or areas of interest:

- *Where and when did you ever feel fully alive? And what were you doing at the time?* Can you remember a time when you were a child and your mother called you to dinner, but you didn't want to go because you were totally absorbed in some project? Today, in what situations do you get so absorbed that time passes very quickly?
- *In what contexts are you able to both give and receive life and love?* Where do you give and receive excitement, enthusiasm, or understanding, caring or compassion, delight, or devotion?
- *Where were you hurt* (shamed, abused, rejected, left behind, silenced, etc.) *and then healed of that hurt?* How did people help you when you hurt? Do you want to help heal people who have been hurt as you were?
- *Are there things you feel you must do, things you "must be about," no matter how difficult, exhausting, or unrewarding they may be?*

God calls you through your desires for good things, through your enthusiasms, your absorptions, your hurts, and your healings. Wherever you are giving and receiving life and love is where God is calling you.

The Call of the Young Jesus: Dialogue (Basic Principle 3)

First Prelude: You might read Luke's story of the divine calling of the young Jesus in the temple (Luke 2:41–52). Or you might imagine the young Jesus in another setting.

Second Prelude: You might like to imagine yourself walking with Jesus, perhaps on the way back to Nazareth from the temple in Jerusalem. The scene is less important than that you have a serious and lengthy dialogue with him as a young person.

Third Prelude: Ask for the grace to understand the dynamics of a divine call and to come to recognize how God has called you to serve in the Christ Project.

1. You might begin your dialogue by asking Jesus how he first
   became aware of his divine calling. Perhaps it happened the
   way Luke described it. Perhaps it happened in a very different context. Ask Jesus to tell you about it. For example,
   ask him:

   - When were you aware of your first call from God?
   - How did you feel after hearing this divine call?
   - How did you respond to it?
   - How did it change your way of thinking about your
     life?
   - Were there other times while you were young when
     you felt called?

Note: When doing a dialogue form of prayer (see Appendix C,
p. 190), you may write out in your journal, as you are experiencing it,
the words of the dialogue—both what you say and what Jesus says.
Your writing will not distract from your prayer state; in fact, it may
deepen your sense of divine presence. Continue the dialogue on this
first point until you feel a sense of closure or completion. Then move
to the second point.

2. Shift the focus from Jesus' calling to your own calling. Start
   the dialogue with Jesus in any way that feels right for you,
   and let the interaction progress in a natural way. Here are
   some questions you might want to ask the young Jesus
   about your own divine calling. Or you may have your own
   questions to ask him:

   - When was the first time God began calling me?
   - What method did God use to attract my attention to
     my destiny?
   - What people did God involve in this process?
   - Can you help me list the steps that God has used in
     bringing me to this day?

Note: Again, it is very helpful to journal the words of the dialogue, both what you say and what Jesus says. Do the journaling as

you experience it. This is a process different from a meditation review, which you may also do afterward.

3. Shift the focus to your present and future. As I discover my call, how can I live it more deeply? Where can I apply that call in a way that enriches, expands, and intensifies my ability to give and receive love and life? Ask Jesus about this. For example, you may begin this part of the dialogue by asking:

• How can I live my call more deeply?

Colloquy: Close the dialogue prayer with some words of gratitude to the young Jesus.

Review: Even though you may have filled a few pages of your journal with dialogue, it is still important to spend time in a review of the prayer experience.

The Incarnation

Understanding Incarnation

God first made creation sacred about fourteen billion years ago at the Big Bang in the first moment of the universe's life. About two thousand years ago, God made creation doubly sacred by a second Big Bang, which was the appearance of Jesus Christ.[3] We might say that the first Big Bang brought us light and life, the second enlightenment. The two are closely related because the two are different forms of incarnation, two different visible expressions of God's creativity and love (Basic Principles 3 and 4).

For Teilhard, God loved unconditionally both his creation and his divine Son. For Teilhard, both the cosmos and the Christ were expressions of God's Word. And the fullest development of both was the work of the Holy Spirit. In this light, the famous lines spoken by Jesus to Nicodemus given in John's Gospel reveal God's unconditional love for both the cosmos and the Christ. "For God so loved the world [*cosmos* or *all creation* in Greek] that he gave his only Son, so that everyone who believes in him may not perish but may have eternal life. Indeed, God did not send the Son into the world [creation] to condemn the world [creation], but in order that the world [creation] might be saved through him." (John 3:16–17).[4]

Incarnation means that a divine being enters into some physical expression or form. That is a basic understanding of this word. If that is so, then incarnation happened first in creation at the beginning of time. According to the creation story revealed by modern science—a new (to us) creation story—the phenomenon of evolution describes God's evolving incarnation into the universe. We have become aware of this gradual evolution through the lens of science, watching creation on Earth change and develop through billions of years. The

---

3. Franciscan sister Ilia Delio, Professor of Spirituality at Washington Theological Union, first suggested this concept in her book *The Humility of God* (p. 60) when she wrote, "Jesus…is the 'Big Bang' of the human potential for God, because in his unique person he realized the created capacity for God" (Cincinnati: St. Anthony Messenger Press, 2005).

4. Because of Teilhard's emphasis on God's unconditional love for creation, he is considered the patron of environmentalists and ecologists, and all those working to save the planet.

revelatory story of this incarnation can now begin to be told in its true evolutionary language.

When this evolutionary process on Earth was ready, or as scripture says "in the fullness of time," it came to a focal point in Jesus, a second and very explicit and personal incarnation. The Word of God chose to unite with earthly matter in new and profoundly personal revelatory ways. "The Word became flesh and lived among us" (John 1:14). Through him, a new understanding of the meaning, purpose, and power of creation passed into the human community.

Why would God want to become a human being? Many traditional answers have been given to this question. But there is also an evolutionary answer.

A primary reason for the incarnation is that God wanted to reveal to us that everything God created in the universe—literally every thing and every process—is sacred and holy and lives in Christ. "In the beginning was the Word.…All things came into being through him, and without him not one thing came into being" (John 1:1, 3).

The divine Word wants to embrace all the elements of the cosmos. He loves humanity so much that he chooses to experience every moment of the human process, from gestation in a mother's womb, birth, childhood, teen years, life in an ordinary family and community. He loved us so much he wanted to have the full human experience, from conception to death. "Though he was in the form of God, he emptied himself…being born in human likeness and being found in human form and became obedient to the point of death" (Eph 2:6–8).

God revealed this divine desire to us first through the physical body of his mother, Mary, beginning on the day of the annunciation.

Although we have developed many doctrinal truths about Jesus Christ, we know very few facts about his historical life, especially about his infancy and childhood. What we do know about his arrival on Earth as historical fact is simply that a person named Jesus of Nazareth was born about two thousand years ago, and his mother's name was Mary.

Although this may seem a severe limitation on your ability to contemplate the events of the annunciation, visitation, and nativity, it is not at all so. On the contrary, it gives you great freedom. It allows you to envision these events in your imagination in any way you wish to picture them. You may follow Matthew's or Luke's descriptions, or you may invent your own version of the events and their contexts. You are invited to personalize the scriptures, which is what Ignatius always invited his retreatants to do. "Something" really happened at the annunciation, visitation, and nativity, and you are free to imagine *how* it happened.

The point of these contemplations is to use your imagination in any way that will nurture in you the religious experiences of wonder, awe, and gratitude. You may begin either with the doctrinal truths of the incarnation or with the scientific truths of evolution.

How to Begin

On the one hand, you may begin with the doctrinal truth that the Word of God chose to become a human being. Allow consideration of this mystery to powerfully evoke wonder and awe in you—and gratitude for the tremendous love God shows to you and to all of us—in this divine choice.

On the other hand, you may begin with the evolutionary scientific information about the genesis and gestation of a human body, and find that this approach likewise evokes a strong experience of wonder and gratitude. The scientific story of human conception and development in the womb carries religious, spiritual, and a miraculous power in itself.

For Teilhard, the mystery of the incarnation permeates the entire history of creation, from the Big Bang to the parousia. Through the process of incarnation, the Divine Word permeates every element and aspect of creation. Through the incarnation of Jesus, the Divine Word enters into and sanctifies every step and stage of the human process. Perhaps the most awesome and mysterious of these processes are those of fetal development and evolutionary recapitulation that happen in the darkness of the mother's womb. In textual commentaries, some of these processes are suggested for your reflection. Use them only to the degree that they are helpful in deepening your reverence for the incarnation.

The scientific and theological approaches cannot be separated from each other, but neither can you put them together without attending to each. God is at work in the evolutionary process, both theologically and scientifically, at all stages. The Christ Project itself, that is, God's eternal plan for creation, emerges out of this evolutionary story of creation. At every moment, whatever is happening to Jesus in the womb is an expression of the Divine Word's love for us. The Divine Word becomes human so that through him we may become divine.

The Holy Spirit drives the whole process. "The Holy Spirit will come upon you, and the power of the Most High will overshadow you" (Luke 1:35).

The Incarnation: Meditation (Basic Principles 6, 14 and 15)

First Prelude: God wants to reveal to humans that all creation is sacred. For Teilhard, creation was made to continue evolving so, in time, it could become conscious of itself and conscious of living in a divine milieu. Creation flowed out from God's infinite love. The Divine Word reveals this truth to us by emerging in his divine nature from within the Earth's evolutionary process at the appointed time in history in human nature as the person Jesus.

Second Prelude: You are free to imagine, as Luke did, the house and garden of Mary, and Gabriel making the announcement. Or you may picture Mary's coming to the awareness of the incarnation in your own way. More importantly, you are encouraged to picture yourself in the scene, perhaps as a close friend of Mary, so that you may converse intimately with her throughout the contemplation.

Third Prelude: Ask for the graces that you need. For example, you may desire the grace to see and understand how God's love is working on your behalf in creation. Or how in Jesus the Divine Word shows that all things are sacred and makes all things one—with him, in him, and through him. You may ask for the grace of wonder and awe at the action of the Divine Word wanting to show his love by choosing to experience every moment of what it means to be a human being.

1. THE ANNUNCIATION

Enter into the scene in any way that feels natural and right for you. For example, as a friend of Mary, you may explain to her (see commentary) what science now knows—and Mary could not have known—about what is happening inside her womb. Listen to how she responds with wonder and surprise at what you tell her. And ask her how, as a woman and mother, she is experiencing these first moments of openness to what God is asking of her. Ask her to tell you about her experience of feeling loved by God. Respond as a close friend.

The following commentaries offer a simple, rather clinical description of the human gestation process. In your contemplation, as you speak to Mary, you may tell her of the beauty and stunning wonder of this amazing fetal evolutionary process and recognize God's creative love at work in it (Basic Principle 1).

Commentary: In Mary, the fertilized ovum immediately began cell division (mitosis). This tiny ball of cells attached itself to the wall of her uterus and began to grow into an embryo. Once this ovum (egg) was fertilized in Mary, the remarkable process of the human development of Jesus began.

2. The Visitation and Mary's Pregnancy

As Mary goes on with her life, carrying out her tasks at home, then (according to Luke) visiting and remaining with Elizabeth for three months, reflect on how the embryo in Mary's womb is quietly transforming into the infant person of Jesus. You may wish to listen as Mary and Elizabeth talk about their babies and bless each other. Or you may simply be with Mary, wherever she happens to be, during the first four months of her pregnancy.

Explain to her, month by month, if you wish, the awesome process that is happening inside her womb, how her divine baby is developing (see commentary). You may also listen as she tells you how she is experiencing her pregnancy and how she talks to God about it. Ask her to teach you how to love God, how to talk to God, and how to be profoundly grateful for the gift of human life.

Commentary: During the nine-month period of gestation in Mary's womb, a series of changes transformed that single fertilized cell into a complex organism made of trillions of cells—to become the human being we know as Jesus of Nazareth.

During the first weeks in Mary's womb, Jesus' nervous system, brain, digestive system, ears, and arms begin to form. At twenty-one days, perhaps on her way to Elizabeth's, his heart takes shape and begins to beat. It is the first beating of the Sacred Heart of Jesus.

During the second month, while she and Elizabeth are waiting for John's birth, Jesus' nostrils, eyelids, nose, fingers, legs, feet, toes, testes, and bones begin to form; his head is as large as his body; his cardiovascular system is fully functional, yet Jesus' body is less than one inch long. It is hard to imagine that Jesus was, at one time, barely one inch long.

During the third month, Jesus' head is still dominant, but his body is lengthening, about 1.5 inches long. Growth of chin and other facial structures give him a human face and profile.

During the period shortly after Elizabeth has given birth to her son John, and throughout Mary's fourth month, Jesus in Mary's womb begins blinking his eyes and sucking his lips; his body begins to outgrow his head; Mary can put her hands on her stomach and feel Jesus' movements for the first time.

3. Mary Returns to Nazareth

Perhaps you can talk with Mary as she is returning home, or after she has returned home to Nazareth. Explain to her how the baby in her womb continues to grow and develop during these final months of her pregnancy (see commentary). Ask her how she relates to her baby now that she can feel him moving around inside her. Ask her how she talks lovingly to him inside her womb. Ask her to tell you what she is learning about God's creativity and God's ways of loving us.

Commentary: By the fifth month, Jesus' limbs are achieving their final proportions; his eyelashes and eyebrows appear; he has grown to about 6.5 inches long.

During the sixth month, Jesus shows a substantial increase in weight; he stretches to about 13 inches long. To anyone observant in the tiny village of Nazareth, Mary is obviously pregnant.

During the seventh month, Jesus in the womb develops fingernails and toenails; he grows to 15–20 inches long.

During the final months, while Jesus is growing and gaining weight, Mary and Joseph will be making the journey to Bethlehem, where Jesus is to be born.

Colloquy: At the close of your reflections, you may speak of your gratitude and wonder at what the incarnation means for all of creation, and ask for the graces you may need to be able to respond adequately to such a loving divine gesture.

Ask for a deepening of the grace to stand in wonder at how God is at work in the evolutionary process of each individual as well as in Jesus. Ask for the grace to see how these scientific facts have religious power, how they supply new form and language to the religious doctrines about incarnation.

Aware of living in the divine milieu, you may direct your prayers to the Creator, the Holy Spirit, the divine Infant, or to Mary. Share what is happening to you with as many of these persons as you wish.

Review: Journal in some detail what happened to you during this contemplation, especially any insights, graces, or strong feelings. It often helps to write out also some of the dialogue that you may have had with Mary during the contemplation, and what went on in your heart during the colloquies. Allow about fifteen minutes for this process.

The Nativity: Meditation (Basic Principle 13)

Since we are so used to seeing and holding newborn babies in our arms, we can miss the opportunity to stand in awe at the marvelous workings that are continually happening inside the skin of each child, workings in "darkness" that we would never know except for the results of modern science.

First Prelude: Luke tells us of the rejoicing of the angels and all the holy people already with God, as Mary gives birth to Jesus and he takes his first breath as a human being.

Second Prelude: See the place where Mary and Joseph are staying and the moment of his birth. Perhaps you can see Joseph looking with longing and concern at Mary, wanting with all his heart for everything to go well. Perhaps the two of them pray together and recite a familiar psalm. Perhaps, if you can picture yourself in the scene, you can make yourself helpful and caring.

Third Prelude: Here ask for the graces you need. Perhaps it is to see and understand God's boundless love for us. Or, how even during Jesus' first few moments of human life and through his first breaths the incarnational process shows that many more things of Earth are explicitly being made sacred. Or how, just by being a human baby, he continues to make all things one—with him, in him, and through him. His little body already contains many of the elements found throughout the cosmos. Or to know of—and experience personally—the boundless love Mary and Joseph have for this special child God has put into their care.

1. Jesus Is Born in Bethlehem

Reflect on, or contemplate, how the newborn Jesus takes his first breath on his own. Picture how Mary looks with deepest love on the body of the child she has given birth to. Imagine yourself standing beside her as you converse together. Perhaps she will ask you to hold the baby. As you describe to Mary what science has learned about human birth and what Jesus taking his first breath implies (see commentary), listen as she describes to you what it means to her to give birth to her son.

Commentary: When Jesus comes forth from Mary, he takes his first breath. With his first breath, Jesus takes as his own, he incarnates—and thereby makes an actual part of himself—the many elements floating around him in the atmosphere and sanctifies them, since they become one with him as he inhales them.

2. Nurturing Jesus' Body

Perhaps, Mary will let you hold the baby in your own arms. As you look at the baby with love, you might explain to Mary some of the wonderful things that have happened inside the complex inner workings of her baby's body. Explain in your own words how, through the food she ate (see commentary), each of these elements of Earth absorbed by the baby's body were being made sacred and holy. Imagine Mary telling you about how it felt when she was eating, knowing that she was helping feed the infant growing within her. Perhaps Mary is nursing the baby, continuing to nourish him with the foods of Earth.

Commentary: Biologists tell us that during pregnancy the placenta facilitates the transfer of nutrients, carbohydrates, proteins, hormones, and other substances from mother to fetus. He is still getting these through his mother's milk.

More than fifty mineral elements would have been incarnated in the healthy human body of Jesus. These are elements of Earth's crust that Jesus, the Word of God—just by eating and consuming— sanctifies them for all eternity in his human body. You have only to study the ingredients printed on the label of your daily vitamin and mineral bottle to see how many of the metals and minerals of Earth's crust were necessary for Jesus to remain a healthy human being.

3. THE GENETIC MATERIAL IN JESUS' BODY

Consider the deep source of the genes of Jesus. His genetic material inherited directly from Mary has a long history, going back perhaps over a hundred thousand years to some first mother in the center of Africa, that in their Hebrew tradition they would call Eve. Try to grasp how Jesus—and you—inherited genes that record a long history through countless generations reaching far back, many millions of years, through the many stages of the hominid line and into the animal kingdom. He, together with all of us, shares this common genetic ancestry.

Mary and Joseph could have known none of this information during their life on Earth. Hear the two of them talk to you about what Jesus' ancestry means to them. To love Jesus is to love all creation, for it is all there in his genetic history, there recorded and made sacred in each cell of his little body.

Commentary: In his DNA, Jesus carries with him the evolving story of how humans became humans (homo sapiens). In his DNA, if we had it to analyze, geneticists assure us we could trace the evolutionary line right back to the first living beings in the sea and on Earth. In having human DNA Jesus incarnates (just as we do) the complete evolutionary phylum in his own being. Even parts of the evolutionary DNA of all the extinct forms of homo sapiens, such as the Neanderthal and homo floresiensis, would leave an imprint and be preserved in Jesus' DNA—as it is in our own DNA. Jesus as a human and we as humans are fundamentally connected with everything that was ever created or has evolved. Furthermore, it is all sacred and unconditionally loved by God.

Colloquy: At the closing of your reflections, perhaps while holding the baby Jesus in your arms and feeling your deep love for him, you may speak of your gratitude and wonder at the wide implications of what it means when we say that Jesus was fully human. Ask for the graces you may need to be able to respond adequately to such a loving gesture of God.

Aware of being in the divine milieu, you may direct your prayers to the Creator, the Holy Spirit, the divine Infant, or to Mary.

Review: In your journal, write in some detail what happened to you during this contemplation, especially any insights, graces, or strong feelings—and, of course, any important dialogue. It often helps to put in writing also what went on in your heart during the colloquies. Allow about fifteen minutes for this process.

The Two Standards

What Are Standards?

In medieval battles, each army fought under the flag or standard of its ruler. The standard-bearer rode into battle at the head of the troops, holding his king's flag aloft. The standard identified the ruler and his people, and what they stood for. Ignatius chose this military imagery of the battle standard around which to build this now-classic meditation. He was of course talking about a spiritual battle. The underlying meaning of *standard*, however, reveals a powerful insight.

The Latin expression *regnum Dei* may be translated either as the "kingdom of God" or the "reign of God." Typically, when people speak of a *kingdom*, they are referring to the territory ruled by a certain king. However, the word *reign* has a different emphasis, not a territorial one. Reign emphasizes rather the goals, plans, policies, practices, or intentions of the ruler during his or her tenure. Thus, we use the expression "during the reign of Julius Caesar" when summarizing what he did while he ruled, or "during the reign of Queen Elizabeth" when saying what she accomplished. Such plans and policies make up the ruler's standard, that is, what the ruler "stands for."

Christ's standard includes those values, beliefs, and principles that represent the reign of Christ. They are expressed, for example, in the Beatitudes and the rest of the Sermon on the Mount. They are in contrast to the values, beliefs, and principles of what Ignatius calls "the enemy." Those are the two standards of this meditation: the standard of Christ and the standard of the enemy (Basic Principle 2).

Teilhard's Version of the Christ Project

Since the beginning of space/time (since the first moment of creation) almost fourteen billion years ago, God the Creator, by his Word, set into motion a divinely-directed cosmic evolutionary project, with its direction governed by the evolutionary Law of Attraction-Connection-Complexity-Consciousness. The aim of this divine evolutionary process, over eons of time, is to make the universe—through us humans—conscious of itself and what it truly is and has always been, namely, the outwardly expressed Word of God.

In this scenario, the task of Christ's workers—those operating under Christ's standard—is to do what they can to help make the whole world realize that it is one Being, loved by God and kept in existence by the Holy Spirit. This one Being is nothing other than the Cosmic Christ, with the entire universe as his Body. Therefore, whoever helps people and the planet develop together in mutual respect, care, love, compassion, and forgiveness is operating under Christ's standard. "Whoever did this to the least of my brothers did it to me" (Matt 25:40).

The complete fulfillment of this Christ Project is obviously a long way off, but whatever positive effects we can accomplish now and during our lifetimes will help move the divine plan one small step closer to its completion. Nothing is ever lost, and no one or nothing is ever outside the divine milieu.

With this fuller understanding of the Christ Project, we can revisit the strategies of Christ and of the enemy.

Revisiting the Strategies

In an evolutionary approach, Christ's reign involves a struggle, not primarily for individual souls, but for the accomplishment of a divine evolutionary project, cosmic in scope. In this view of the divine project, Christ and his workers are the proactive force, and the enemy is on the defensive. The enemy's best strategy is to try to sabotage, upset, damage, and disrupt the progress of this divine plan so that it never succeeds. However, Christ assures us that it will ultimately succeed. He is putting his trust in us.

While the Christ Project is operating primarily at an organic and collective level, concerned with the evolutionary transformation of the whole of creation, each individual person always remains a distinctly identifiable and integral part of the plan. All sentient beings, individually and collectively, are inextricably connected to each other and to everything else in the universe. Ultimately, when the Christ Project reaches its fulfillment, each being will recognize that it is and has always been a unique unit or "cell" in the cosmic Body of Christ. Each human will rejoice, not so much for having passed the test and made it into heaven, but primarily for being fully conscious that it lives and moves and has its being in Christ, and will continue to enjoy that beatific consciousness for all eternity.

The Two Standards: Meditation (Basic Principle 9)

First Prelude: Today, Christ, through members of his Body on Earth, has the task of enrolling workers to commit themselves to the Christ Project.

Second Prelude: Imagine Christ himself among a group of contemporary people, speaking now to each one individually, and then to the whole group, about his plans and worldwide project. You approach the group to listen because you really want to understand what he is about.

Third Prelude: Here it will be to ask for the grace to truly understand what Christ is trying to do in the world, to get a deep sense of what his standard represents, and the different ways you might play a part in his work. Ask not only to understand the policies and plans of Christ and how you can best fit into them, but also to become familiar with the specific tactics the enemy is using to detour you from your commitment to Christ.

Part One: Christ's Standard

1. CHRIST SPEAKS TO YOU

The proof that people are committed to the Christ Project and engaged in it is, first of all, measured by their attitude and behavior toward the poor, the sick, the grieving, the lonely, the forgotten, the discouraged, the dispossessed, the innocent, the frightened, the disenfranchised, etc. Christ's Sermon on the Mount (Matt 5:1–15) is the primary manifesto of Christ's standards.

You may hear in your heart Christ saying something like this directly to you:

> If you wish to follow me, to live and work under my standard, here is what I will look for from you.
>
> Are you willing to be poor in spirit, that is, to realize how much more you need to grow in realizing who you are called to become?
>
> Are you willing to learn to mourn and deal with loss and failure in your own life, as well as how to comfort people who are grieving?

Are you willing to be gentle, docile, and unassuming, for you will be required often to show compassion to the lost and forgotten, the poor and the sick, the anxious and the discouraged?

Are you willing to be continually merciful and forgiving toward others—even toward your enemies and toward yourself?

Are you willing to be open and pure in heart, for only then will you be able to recognize my presence in the least likely places?

Are you also willing to be a peacemaker, willing to keep searching to find ways to mutual understanding with others and defending the innocent without resorting to violence?

I am looking for men and women who hunger and thirst for honesty and truth and are willing to take a stand against injustice.

I am looking for men and women who expect to be persecuted for being good, honest, and compassionate, and who will not be surprised to be scorned falsely and hear all kinds of evil spoken against them on my account.

In addition, I am looking for you to be proactive and creative, to be the salt of the earth, never losing your taste for the kingdom.

I am looking for you to be a lamp for the world, letting God's light shine through you, so that others may see the good works around them and give glory to the Creator.

Can you be these things for me?

Can you believe that I am always with you, even in the direst poverty or the deepest grief?

Can you believe that even when you are persecuted or rejected by others, you will have all the grace you need to grow and to do your task?

You may respond from your heart to any or all of these statements of Christ.

2. CHRIST SPEAKS TO THE GROUP OF HIS WORKERS

After you have dialogued with Christ, you notice that he turns to speak to the whole group of his workers, saying:

> Those who are committed to this project will strive to use all their energy, talents, and skills to promote the evolutionary process wherever they can. There are tens of thousands of small and large projects already under way that are, consciously or unconsciously, building the Body of Christ.
>
> Some are doing research that directly affects the evolutionary process technologically, biologically, socially, psychologically, or spiritually.
>
> Others are working at forms of interfaith and ecumenical unity.
>
> Others are working to reduce various kinds of discrimination.
>
> Others are caring for the uncared-for.
>
> Others are working ecologically to save Earth itself. And so on.
>
> Those who are not against us are with us (see Mark 9:40).
>
> My purpose is to push the evolutionary project toward ever-higher levels of consciousness, and to do it using the intrinsic power of love, always including and caring for the poor, the lonely, the sick, the grieving, and those who have been left behind and forgotten.

You can always give and receive love and life no matter where you are, no matter how you feel, and no matter what the situation is.

3. YOU ASK CHRIST HOW YOU ARE TO DO THIS, AND HE ANSWERS

You and the other workers turn to Christ and ask him how you are to carry out his wishes. He replies:

> You ask me how you can do this. Here is a way.

If you wish to follow me, make yourself attractive and approachable—warm, thoughtful, affirming, sympathetic, interesting—so you can build connections—friendships, associations, teams, and committees—groups that will help build unity among people.

Invite complexity into your life—build new relationships, assume new responsibilities, challenge yourself, recreate yourself, be open to those who do not think the way you do—so that you are forced to grow, develop, and become more conscious of who you are and what you can become. Invite complexity into the lives of others so that they may become more conscious of who they are and of their potential for service.

Let helping build the Body of Christ on Earth become your primary purpose and meaning in life. As a committed loving person, you may trust me to take care of your eternal soul.

Can you do this for me and with me?

First Colloquy: With Our Lady—I will ask her that her Son and Lord be pleased to accept me under his standard. I pray for the grace that helping develop the Body of Christ on Earth will be my primary purpose. To this end, I will focus my energies on using the Law of Attraction-Connection-Complexity-Consciousness. I will make myself attractive in body, mind, and spirit. I will build connections with others who share this purpose. I will invite complexity into my life. I will strive to become more and more conscious of who I am and of my potential for service. (End with a Hail Mary.)

Note: It is not surprising that many will find it difficult and frightening to make such a radical commitment to serve under the Lord's standard, once they truly begin to understand all that it might entail. Ignatius understood this very well. If a person at least "wishes" he or she had the generosity and courage to make such a commitment, Ignatius suggests that they take a step back and begin the colloquy by asking for the grace "to have the desire to desire" to make such a commitment.

Second Colloquy: With Christ—I will ask him to accept me under his standard. I will make some of the same affirmations as in the colloquy with Our Lady. I affirm that I will use my energy and creativity to help the Body of Christ grow in consciousness within my various spheres of influence. I will prove that I am committed to this Christ Project and engaged in it by my loving attitude and behavior toward the poor, the sick, the grieving, the lonely, the discouraged, the dispossessed, the disenfranchised, etc. I will trust that, being in Christ's service, he will keep my soul safe. Speak to Christ from your heart.

Third Colloquy: With the Creator—I will ask God who is Lord of Creation to bless my choice to serve under his Son's standard. I will express my gratitude to the Creator for giving us his Son as a guide and head of creation's body. I will express my gratitude for being able to "read" God's holy revelation in the "book" of creation. I will praise God for the evolutionary law of love implanted in every particle of creation. I will learn to use this evolutionary energy to promote the glory of God. (End with the Our Father.)

Part Two: The Enemy's Strategy

1. THE ENEMY'S TACTICS

Jesus referred to Satan as the enemy or the destroyer. The enemy is whatever or whoever is trying to destroy what God is building. Whether you choose to imagine the enemy as certain human beings or a group of individual spiritual beings such as devils, or as an impersonal kind of destructive, devolutionary power or inertial energy, it does not matter. The experiential fact is that there appear to be negative and damaging forces at work among us.

You may hear Christ say to you:

The enemy is trying to undermine and destroy this divine project. Here are several ways the enemy may work to subvert and sabotage it.

The enemy can chip away at the Christ Project by getting people—especially influential people—preoccupied with becoming rich and powerful and then seducing them to become totally self-absorbed in their own greed, power, and pride—or in the absorbing task of managing their own riches. So, be wary of this tactic.

But in this day, the enemy may be much more successful in a number of other ways. It is for you and each person to discover how the enemy is infiltrating and undermining you and the groups you are in.

The enemy's first and easiest tactic is to get people to avoid becoming "conscious." For example, the enemy can keep people distracted by—and even addicted to—mindless entertainment, games, and amusements; or keep them absorbed in busywork with shopping, building a career, and paying bills; or focus them on keeping the status quo and not making any waves. This way people stay unconscious of God's project.

The enemy can also beset humans with the ancient, yet ever new, demons—worry, doubt, fears, guilt, apathy, and laziness. Any of these will keep people from putting full effort into the work of the kingdom.

Another easy way to hinder God's work is for the enemy to get people to avoid involvement in any human project that might help the Christ Project. Here the enemy can easily get people to play the bystander, the victim, the cynic, the complainer, the indecisive one, or the pessimist. There are many who'd rather not make any contributions.

Another easy way to hinder God's work is for the enemy to offer people a variety of excuses to keep from getting involved in anything that might do good in the world. Here, the enemy gets people to say things like "It's too dangerous," "I'm too busy," "It's too much trouble," "I'd rather stay out of it," or "There's nothing in it for me."

It is a popular but powerfully true saying, "All that is necessary for the triumph of evil is for good people to do nothing."

Another enemy strategy is to lead people away from hard work and human effort by convincing them of the supreme importance of their own comfort and safety, that they are entitled to being treated as a very important person, and that they should not commit themselves to anything that might make them uncomfortable.

How does the enemy work on you?

According to Father Ron Rolheiser, "American culture is the most powerful narcotic this planet has ever perpetrated."[5] By keeping us focused on food, pleasure, entertainment, and comfort, it keeps us from developing spiritual depth, personal integrity, character, concern for the poor, or community life.

2. THE COST OF COMMITMENT

Picture Christ calling you aside and saying words like these to you.

> You can be sure that a commitment to the Christ Project will have its costs in terms of effort and long hours, perhaps much of it unappreciated or even laughed at. And you will be continually tempted by the enemy.
> Is this the life you really want?
> Are you really willing to follow me and live according to my standard?

Colloquy: You may repeat each of the three colloquies following the First Part of this meditation—one to Our Lady, a second to Christ, and a third to the Creator. Speak to each of them from your own heart and in your own words.

Review: It is important to journal how this meditation went for you, where during it you felt movements of generosity, and where you felt resistance to the call, fear, or even revulsion. How and where do you think you are being called to work in the Christ Project? Which of the enemy's strategies are likely to have an impact on you? Where are your weak points?

Note: Because this is a key meditation in the New Spiritual Exercises, you may repeat the Two Standards meditation once or twice more during the day.

---

5. *National Catholic Reporter*, August 17, 2007.

Three Pairs of People

Beyond the Two Standards Meditation

In the Kingdom meditation, you were invited to make a generous commitment to work alongside Christ in helping bring the divine Christ Project to completion, for it is an evolving project and will not be fully completed until the end of time.

In the Two Standards meditation you were presented with the new mind-set needed to succeed in working for the Project. Now, Ignatius invites you to take one developmental step further (Basic Principle 11). What would you do in the following test case?

Three Pairs of People: A Consideration

A Test Case

Imagine you came into a windfall of money—nothing you earned. It fell into your lap. Let's say you won the lottery and were awarded ten million dollars.

Ignatius asks you to reflect on three different classes of people—actually three pairs of people—and how they might deal with this good fortune. He wonders in which of the three classes you might feel most at home. In doing this consideration, imagine a dialogue going on between you and your partner with whom you are to share the lottery winnings, talking over what you could do with this money.

Ground Rules

Ignatius also sets some ground rules.

First, assume that none of the people pairs in the story wants to lose their eternal souls. Therefore, they are not talking here about using the money to live a life of greed, debauchery, or crime.

Also, assume that all three pairs understand the Divine Project, its basic principles and attitudes, how it operates, what it entails, and they have made a fundamental choice to working toward its successful outcome.

Note: This "consideration" is not treated as a formal meditation but as a situation to read and mull over throughout the day. Please journal your thoughts as you reflect.

Before you begin, you may wish to remind yourself that you are enveloped in the presence of God, who loves you unconditionally, and formulate a preparatory prayer, asking that you may more deeply understand yourself through these considerations. To achieve this clear self-understanding, Ignatius would ask you to pray for the grace of freedom and objectivity, to see yourself as you would truly respond in this situation.

It may feel uncomfortable to discover that you are most at home in the mind-set of the first pair or the second pair, but this is precisely the grace that Ignatius wants for you: to see yourself as you are. Only when you see yourself realistically, can you hope to grow and evolve.

The First Pair

The first pair treats the lottery winnings as a gift to themselves, a true bonus, something to be enjoyed personally and used in any way they might like. They see the money as given to them and belonging to them. Ignatius might say they have an attachment to it. They never get around to asking God how God might want them to act regarding the money. They see it as "their windfall," separate from and not at all connected to the Christ Project or their work for the kingdom.

We may assume that this first pair might spend the money on things like a new home, a new car, new clothing, new equipment, and world travel. They might also invest some of the money, so that it would generate additional income for future needs or wants. They might generously give some of it to their parents, their children, close relatives, or friends. They might agree to fund their children's or grandchildren's education and make down payments on first homes for them. The money would be well spent, not wasted, but it would be spent on themselves and their families. Meantime, they are still committed to the Christ Project.

Individually, their prayer to God simply tells God what they have decided to do with the winnings. They are not looking for God's approval or disapproval. It might be as follows:

I have led a good life and worked hard all my days to praise and glorify you, God. I see winning the lottery as a blessing from you. It is a clear sign that you want me to relax and enjoy myself for the rest of my life. I will prudently invest some of it so that it may gain interest and never fail me and provide a guaranteed income for me and my children and grandchildren. I will enjoy life and give you thanks each day. I will spend time in the Holy Land, where your son came to Earth. I will also use some of the winnings to buy gifts for all my family and friends and to contribute to some charitable causes.

Reflection: Open to a fresh page of your journal and, assuming the mentality of this first pair of people, list how you as one of this pair might spend or invest the ten million dollars that has come to the two of you. See how well or how naturally you fall into this class.

The Second Pair

The second pair of people who won the ten million dollar lottery is very committed to the Christ Project. They want to make a positive difference in the world. They sit down and discuss how they will allocate their winnings. Perhaps they will give some to groups working with the poor and homeless, they might give some to scientific research in fields of consciousness and learning, they might give some to ecological research. The point here is that these two are totally committed to promoting the great Christ Project of achieving the oneness of humankind and of the planet. It is important to this pair that they acknowledge that the money came to them as a gift from God to be used for the Christ Project. The money has been entrusted to them and they will use all of it for the project, but they remain in control of how it is used and distributed. In summary, they figure out on their own how to deal with the money, and then ask God to bless their autonomous choice ("bending God's will to theirs" is the way Ignatius put it).

The prayer of an individual in the second pair might be as follows:

I have led a good life and worked hard all my days. Yet, I have always wanted to make a difference in the world, not just to avoid sin but to do something positive, to make a contribution that would improve life on the planet, and I see this as a chance to do just that. Therefore, I want to use my winnings to help make the world a better place. I'm sure, God, that's exactly what you want. So, I am going to put this money to good use in my favorite causes and research projects. I am excited that the money will be to promote your divine project. I believe you have great plans for us and for all of your creation. I believe there is something immense that you are trying to accomplish on Earth, and I am sure my choices promote your plans. I trust that you will approve and bless my choices and decisions.

Reflection: In the mentality of this second pair of people committed to the Christ Project, list in your journal how you as one of this pair might allocate the ten million dollars that has come to the two of you. These allocations might include programs, charities, and initiatives of your choice—all of which would directly promote the Christ Project. See how well or how naturally you fall into this class.

The Third Pair

The third pair of people who won the ten million dollar lottery is also committed to the Christ Project, but they see their winning differently from the first two pairs. (Many will find it difficult to see that there could be anyone more deeply committed to the Christ Project than the second pair. But Ignatius assures us that there is.)

The first couple saw the money as a special personal blessing given exclusively to them to be used for their own personal happiness and enjoyment and of those near and dear to them.

The second couple saw the money as a gift from God to them, not to further their own personal happiness and enjoyment, but to further the Christ Project. However, this second couple wants to keep to themselves the power to make the decision how and where to allocate the gift of money.

The third couple sees the money as belonging to God, not to themselves. They are merely God's instruments in using or distributing the money. They are anxious to find out how God wants it allocated, and will not spend or give away any of it until they find out God's will for it.

In their prayer, they ask for the grace to be free enough interiorly, first, to desire to know God's will in the matter, second, to pray to choose to accede to that will, and third, to carry out that will, once known, because it is God's will and for no other reason.

They say to each other something like this:

> How does God want us to use this money? This money belongs to God. We are merely instruments of God's love and healing in the world. We must discern what God wants done with this money. Perhaps God wants us to allocate it the way we would personally like to allocate it, but perhaps God has totally other plans for it. We will not do anything until we can discern what God wants.

Reflection: Considering the mentality of the third pair, how well do you fit into this couple's way of dealing with the lottery winnings?

Colloquy: After your reflection on the three pairs of people, speak to Christ about how you are feeling, what your concerns are, and perhaps what you are fearful of or anxious about with respect to these three levels of response.

Review: Your task is to reflect on these three classes of people and their prayer, and to discover which class you belong to and which class you would like to belong—and why? Write your responses in your journal.

Note: This consideration is presented to help you see where among these three classes of people you most naturally fit. No matter which of the three classes you may fall into, God can use whatever you do to further the Christ Project.

Four Levels of Service

This consideration on the Four Levels of Service is a variation of Ignatius' consideration on the Three Degrees of Humility.[6] Both considerations explore the same issue, namely, the level of docile generosity and open-ended commitment a retreatant is ready to offer Christ. However, an evolutionary spirituality creates a much broader context for these levels of service, especially when the Christ Project is more clearly defined and the Law of Attraction-Connection-Complexity-Consciousness identified. It shows how the value of each person's human effort to make the world a better place is tremendously enlarged and enriched.

Whether we know it or not, we are all employed in God's service while we live on Earth. That is, we are destined—willingly or unwillingly—to be involved in God's purposes.

Most people, however, live in what social scientists call a cultural trance—that is, most people, even many people of faith, are not "awake" enough to recognize and realize that God has a vast plan for us humans and for all of creation. Such people may believe different things. Some have been taught by the culture to believe that the purpose of life is to pursue personal happiness. Still others have been taught to believe that life is all about achievement: amassing money and possessions, striving for upward mobility, or obtaining power or authority and control over others, etc. From the perspective of an evolutionary faith, all of these people are spiritually "asleep," and do not recognize their true purpose for being born and living on Earth.

In considering the following four degrees of service, you are to assume a number of things:

> First, that each person in these stories, unquestionably, loves Jesus Christ.
> Second, that each one wants to serve God faithfully and live with God forever.
> Third, that each one wishes that all people experience the fullness of life with God forever.

---

6. In Ignatius' day, the Latin *humilitas*, the word Ignatius uses in his text, might be better translated as "docility or openness to God's will for me." For Ignatius, for example, Mary's *yes* to be the mother of Jesus would be an expression of *humilitas*.

Fourth, that each person being described is *not* living in a cultural trance but is conscious of what God is trying to do in the world, namely, to bring about the conscious oneness of the planet—"that all may be one"—the Christ Project.

Nevertheless, people respond in four different degrees or levels of generosity and involvement. The four case studies may help you to see at which level you are at present and to which level you aspire.

It is perfectly acceptable for you to be at any of the four levels at present. And it is wise to be honest about where you truly are. The invitation here is to follow Christ and aspire to a higher level of generosity and involvement.

Four Levels of Service: A Consideration (Basic Principle 9)

Preparation: This consideration is not treated as a formal meditation but rather as case studies to read and mull over throughout the day. As you begin, you may wish to place yourself in the presence of God and formulate a preparatory prayer, asking that you may more deeply understand yourself through these considerations.

Context: The following describe four levels of service found among those working in God's organization on Earth to accomplish the Christ Project.

1. THE SELF-FOCUSED SERVANT

The typical self-focused servant of God (There have been many priests, bishops, cardinals, popes, and laypeople in this level.) might say to himself or herself:

I know how to use a system—including the church's system—to my advantage. I'll do the work I'm required to do, but I'll make sure I have enough time to have a lot of fun and pursue my own interests. I know how to inspire others to work energetically. I'll see that my reports and accomplishments are recognized. I'll be outspoken for God's cause and make sure that others recognize that I am a committed servant of God. Deep down, I want God's great project to succeed. I really do. And I don't think I am standing in the way of its success, since God is all-powerful. Furthermore, I long with all my heart to enjoy heaven with Jesus, eternally.

2. THE OBEDIENT SERVANT

The typical obedient servant of God might say to himself or herself:

I keep all the commandments. I avoid sin. I obey my superiors. I follow the rules. I stay out of trouble, and I'm not a troublemaker. I do my job without complaining. And I do a good job with no slacking. I even tolerate the boring tasks that are part of my job. I even volunteer for extra hours, but I prefer not to try something new or go out on a limb. I want to remain safe and secure in my faith. I prefer to do what I am duty-bound to do. I am proud to be part of the great project that God is accomplishing, and I am proud to be doing what I have been asked to do. I long with all my heart to enjoy heaven with Jesus, eternally.

3. THE LOYAL SERVANT

The typical loyal servant of God might say:

If I do everything I am expected to do, I feel I am not really being generous enough with my loving God. So I often volunteer to do more. At times, I may ask to be assigned a thankless task or a job where I am likely, to have to deal with angry and unhappy people. When I think of Jesus who willingly suffered and died for me, I might agree to do tasks where I might be misunderstood or laughed at by others. I do it because I see these tasks as involved in furthering the work of God's project on Earth. Of course, it can be exhausting, stressful, and often frustrating. It may even require pain and suffering. When I am asked to do something, even if it feels repulsive or dangerous, I try to say yes.

And I carry out the task to the best of my ability all for the love of God. I hope I can do it willingly and cheerfully without complaint, just as Jesus did. And I long with all my heart to enjoy heaven with Jesus, eternally.

4. THE PROACTIVE SERVANT

The typical proactive servant of God might say to himself or herself:

I have a glimpse of what God is trying to accomplish in the world, so I choose to focus all my talents and skills and ingenuity in furthering that great cause. I am eager to do all I can and to get others to join the cause. So, when I see an opportunity for improvement in myself or in a process I'm involved in, I will take the initiative. Since the human race is supposed to be growing and becoming more conscious of its divine purpose, I will continue to challenge the status quo, to find ways, working with others, to improve the quality of the products I help make and the services that I perform. I want to grow in knowledge, grace, and consciousness and help others to do the same. I want to find joy in my work and in devising new ways to further God's purpose on Earth. I want to keep stimulating growth in myself and union with others, until the day I die. Then I want to keep working at the divine project even when I am in heaven. In this project there is no such thing as retirement.

Reflection: Your task is to reflect on these four degrees of service and the prayer of each, and to discover which degree of service you would like to offer God—and why. In a colloquy, you may wish to express a renewal of your love and commitment to Jesus Christ.

Conclude your prayerful consideration by reflecting on three important questions. Write your answers in your journal.

- What have I done so far in my life to further God's purposes on Earth?

- What am I presently doing to further God's purposes on Earth?
- What will I do in the future to further God's purposes on Earth?

Note: You may not identify with any of the four case studies presented in this consideration. If so, please write in your journal why you do not identify with any of the four. Your challenge then is to create your own personal prayer that matches the level of generosity and involvement that you are at now. Be sure to record it in your journal.

Jesus' Baptism in the Jordan

Why did Jesus choose to be baptized when it seemed he didn't have to? And why is God the Father so pleased with Jesus getting baptized?

The scriptures don't give us answers to those very important questions. One source of an answer to the question—Why did Jesus choose to be baptized?—is found in the original Greek version of the Baptist's message. In the Latin text and English translations, it says John's baptism is a baptism of repentance, which focuses on *past* deeds or misdeeds. But in the Greek, the word used instead of *repentance* is *metanoia*, which means putting on a new mind-set. *Metanoia* focuses on the way you will now begin thinking and behaving. *Metanoia* implies a *future* orientation.

If Jesus heard this second version of John's message—the *metanoia*, or change of thinking—Jesus could very well accept baptism, because in this meaning baptism is calling for a change in the way Jesus has been thinking about himself and doing things up until now.

Up to this point, Jesus had been living a private, quiet life in Nazareth, the life of a rather normal person. Now he was feeling the call to begin living formally and publicly in promoting the kingdom of God. He was hearing the call of the Baptist to "change the way you are thinking and doing things so that you are more fully supporting the kingdom of God."

The Baptist's Message Today

Today, perhaps more than ever, we see *metanoia* happening. For example, we see movie stars involved in caring for the poor and promoting issues of social justice. Some actresses are auctioning off gowns they wore to the Academy Awards for tens of thousands of dollars and donating the money to various children's charities. Sports stars in our day, in greater numbers than ever before, are using some of their high salaries to create and fund programs for inner-city kids, broken families, single mothers, orphans, and ways to reduce violence and drug addiction. Famous rock musicians are finding ways to bring education, food, medicines, and safe drinking water to poor African villages. All of these people are trying to make a better future.

115

But it is not just the famous people who are experiencing these radical changes of heart and action. It's happening among ordinary people all over the world. Mothers, fathers, businesspeople, and even young people in unprecedented numbers are feeling the call to conversion, to being of service to others—and in our age of individualism, this commitment to service is a true conversion. Some gather to collect food and clothing for the poor and undernourished. Other groups volunteer to help build homes for the homeless and indigent. Others take time out of their normal schedule to serve in soup kitchens or thrift stores. Others provide summer camps for inner city children. Others focus their energies on protecting the environment. Still others form groups to lobby Congress on behalf of those who have no political voice.

Much of this work dedicated to overcoming the forces of *devo-lution* is invisible to the public, yet there are well over a million groups in the world supporting themselves and working to make a positive difference in the lives of others. The Baptist's call to conversion of heart is being heard today in the hearts of people in every country of the world. These people want to change the world and make it a better place.

In this meditation you are invited to hear the message of the Baptist in your own mind and heart, and to respond generously to it, as did Jesus, Ignatius, and the millions of people who have given their time, talents, and money to initiate and carry out causes, locally and worldwide, which promote peace, compassion, social justice, and the gradual forward evolution of society.

The Baptism of Jesus: Meditation and Dialogue (Basic Principle 8)

First Prelude: You may picture in your imagination the scene of John baptizing people in the Jordan River. Perhaps there are many people waiting in line, perhaps only a few. John has just finished preaching his message to the audience: "Change your mind and heart because the Kingdom of God is present." He is saying, in effect, "Change the way you are thinking and doing things in such a way that you are now supporting what God is trying to do in the world." With this in your mind, add the following image.

Second Prelude: Here you may picture in your imagination Jesus walking on his way to John's baptismal site at the Jordan, perhaps still a distance away. Imagine yourself walking beside him asking many questions and listening to his answers.

Third Prelude: Ask for the grace to know the mind and heart of Jesus more deeply, in order to understand more clearly God's future vision for creation as Jesus sees it. You may also ask to love Christ more ardently, and to follow his way of thinking and acting more closely and more generously.

1. WALKING TO THE JORDAN RIVER

Picture yourself walking alongside Jesus asking him the questions that are in your mind and heart. You want to understand the way he thinks as deeply as you can. From understanding him flows love for him.

As in the dialogue prayer form, during this prayer you may write your questions to Jesus in your journal as you ask them, and write his responses as he gives them to you. As in any dialogue, you may discover that Jesus will also ask you questions and expect you to reply.

Note: In preparing for this meditation, you may begin to list some of the questions that arise in your mind, so that when you begin your dialogue you already have a number of questions you wish to ask. You want to know how he thinks and feels and how he makes decisions in more detail. Here are a few sample questions others have wished to ask Jesus as he approached the Jordan River that day:

- *What are some of the factors that influenced you to come to see John?* Did your mother tell you stories about him? Was your father Joseph's death an important factor? Did the rabbi in your village influence you? Did you have any friends who had visited and heard John the Baptist speak? Did you feel an unmistakable inner call to go to the Jordan River?
- *Why are you leaving Nazareth now?* Have you been receiving messages from your heavenly Father recently? What was it that finally—at age thirty—called you away from Nazareth?

- *In Nazareth, did you already have an inkling from your heavenly Father about his great plan and project for you and for all of us—this grand universal future?* Was it this that called you away?
- What was your last conversation with your mother like? *How did you explain to her what you were planning to do? What did you say? What did she say?*
- *What is going on in your mind now?* What are you concerned about? Your mother? Your future?
- *How do you think your life will change if you go through with this baptism?*
- *Are you planning to go right to John immediately and ask to be baptized?* Do you plan to watch him and listen to him for a while—maybe even a day or two—before you step into the river?
- *Is it really necessary for you to meet with John and be baptized before you begin your own ministry?*
- According to the story as John's Gospel tells it, the Baptist knew that the Savior was there among the crowd, but he did not know for sure that you were the one. *Is this the way it was?*

Note: Asking questions has proved to be the most powerful tool in human evolution. Asking questions elicits dialogue and connection. Asking questions and the search for answers create complexity in your life and open your consciousness to new levels.

2. THE DECISION TO BE BAPTIZED

As you and Jesus arrive at the place where John is baptizing, continue to ask questions of Jesus, for you wish to enter his mind and heart if you are to be one of his followers. As you create the scene, listen to what John has to say and observe the many different kinds of people who come to John to be baptized. Some come with a true change of heart. Some come only to watch with curiosity, others to observe with suspicion and jealousy of John's popularity.

Let us suppose Jesus pauses to listen to John preaching. You may ask Jesus some questions as they come to your mind. Here are some sample questions others have wanted to ask Jesus, if you can't think of any of your own:

- How are you being affected by John's preaching?
- Have you ever considered becoming one of John's disciples?
- Did you ever, before now, feel called to do preaching and baptizing as John is doing?
- Does listening to John and observing his work clarify anything for you and for what you were called to do?
- Were you aware before you arrived here that John was proclaiming your presence (and not someone else) as being "the one who is to come after me"?
- Why did you decide to get baptized?

Note: For Jesus to begin preaching and baptizing the way John did would be a radically new way for Jesus to begin thinking and behaving, after thirty years of living a hidden life in Nazareth. We know from Matthew's Gospel that at the beginning of his public ministry Jesus simply imitated John. Jesus preached John's basic message, almost word for word, and baptized people the way John did (see Matt 4:17).

3. Receiving God's Approval

After the Holy Spirit descended on Jesus and God's words of approval were spoken, you may continue to dialogue with Jesus or with John the Baptist.

If you choose to dialogue with Jesus, you may continue to ask him questions, for example:

- What has changed in your mind and heart after the experience of the baptism and hearing the words of your Father?
- Do you have any plans about what to do now that you have committed to change your way of thinking and behaving, which was confirmed by your choice to be baptized?

- Please tell me if you have any plans for me—and show them to me.

Colloquy: You may express your gratitude to God at how God leads each of us—including his Son—to our calling through the words and actions and example of other people. Thank God for sending people into your path to help guide you into your contributions to God's evolutionary work in the world. You may also ask for the grace of generosity, that is, to do more and better things to transform the world on behalf of the Christ Project.

Review: Read over your dialogue—questions and answers—that you have recorded in your journal, and summarize what you have learned about Jesus' process of moving toward a change of mind and heart and how it might apply in your own life and work.

The Baptism of Jesus: A Repetition

FIRST OPTION: STANDARD REPETITION

Some may find that they spend an entire hour of prayer time on just the first point or the first and second points of this dialogue prayer. In such cases, a closing colloquy should be carried out at the end of the prayer time, and the exercise reviewed as usual. In such a case, during a repetition of this exercise, you may begin by starting at the point where you left off in the first hour. Or you may begin at the first point again, especially if you find you have more questions to ask Jesus.

SECOND OPTION: JESUS AND THE PRINCIPLE AND FOUNDATION

An alternative way of repeating this exercise is to dialogue with Jesus about how in his baptism he is coming to recognize and live out the Principle and Foundation. Here, you may choose to take each sentence of the Principle and Foundation and ask Jesus how it applies to him, and then how it might apply to you. End with a colloquy with Jesus or God the Father.

The Temptations of Jesus in the Desert

It is clear that in this event, in this confrontation between Jesus and Satan, Jesus is dealing with something more than a few ordinary temptations. What is at stake here is cosmic in scope, namely, the future of humankind.

In his choice to begin a public ministry, Jesus runs up against a series of obstacles and potential detours to his commitment. But they are not simple obstacles. The first obstacle that would subvert his mission right from the start is his temptation encounter with Satan in the desert. All three Synoptic Gospels report it (Matt 4:1–11, Mark 1:12–13, Luke 4:1–13).

Satan clearly recognizes Jesus and his mission as a threat to evil's growing domination of the world, and Satan will do all he can to distract and detour Jesus from his public mission even before he begins it. You have met this demonic figure before in the meditations on the Kingdom and the Two Standards. Whether or not Satan is a specific being is perhaps less important than the "worldly" values and beliefs he embodies.

Satan and the Spirit of Domination

Here, the character of Satan represents the spirit of domination that permeates the entire world. This is the all-pervasive destructive spirit (or mind-set) people have felt since the beginnings of civilization. This spirit of domination reaches into and infects the economy, politics, science, art, communication, and even religion. This domination system "is characterized by unjust economic relations, oppressive political relations, biased race relations, patriarchal gender relations, hierarchical power relations, and the use of violence to maintain them all."[7] Satan, who represents the primal force of entropy—the heavy downward spiral—on Earth, is the main promoter of this domination mentality. In it, the rich and the rulers dominate all the rest of society.

---

7. Walter Wink, *The Powers That Be: Theology for a New Millennium* (New York: Doubleday, 1998), 39.

Jesus' Experience

This is the domination myth that Jesus grew up with and what he faces in his temptations and repeatedly throughout his ministry. It is the myth his Jewish religious leaders and teachers promulgated and tried even to put into the mouth of God. In his youth, Jesus heard the domination myth in a hundred different ways: that money, health, and power are signs of divine approval and so the wealthy, healthy, and powerful were meant to dominate the weak, the sick, the poor, the widows. The dominators were to use violence to exert their power. Men were to dominate women. Free men were to dominate slaves. Jesus grew up experiencing the oppressive Roman rulers and soldiers who lived out this myth and foisted it upon the Jewish people. Jesus watched his own oppressed people buy into this myth, and with it oppress themselves.

Each of the three temptations is a subtle invitation to Jesus to join the ranks of the dominators, the rich and powerful, the highly respected, the creators of the violence myths that perpetuate their power. Satan recognized that Jesus was a person who could be tremendously influential, and it would be good to have him on the side of the wealthy and powerful.

Jesus, in utter contrast, remains standing on the side of the poor, the infirm, the mentally ill, the slaves, the sinners, the outcasts, the aliens, the rejected, children, and oppressed women. In other words, he is representing an unconditionally loving and compassionate God.

A Teilhard Perspective

Teilhard would probably recast Jesus' temptation experience in the framework of activities and passivities. Activities and passivities, for Teilhard, are deeply cosmological forces. They are complementary and reciprocal structures of life and energy. Understanding these active and passive primal forces gives us an insight into how the universe took shape, how societies took shape, and how our individual lives took shape as well.

Activities are those acts we consciously initiate in order to make an impact on our world. In contrast, *passivities* are what we must endure as we try to make our impact on the world. Passivities include what is given to us, imposed on us, and done to us. Our passivities comprise the events and actions over which we have little or no control, yet which influence us and shape our lives. Whether we like them or not, we must live with our passivities and deal with them, if we want to pursue our purpose and goals in life.

For example, being born into a society permeated by the domination system and its belief in peace through violence is a passivity that powerfully affects all of us. We cannot avoid dealing with it. Similarly, we are all also born into a society where money is worshipped and treated as the only valid measure of self-worth and self-esteem. That is another passivity we must all deal with, if we each hope to pursue our life purpose effectively.

The spirit of domination and the myth of redemptive violence are perhaps the most pervasive passivities of diminishment for the entire human race and the entire physical order. Even though this myth of the "goodness of violence" is something invisible, it lives in the minds and hearts of people. As such, it is very real. It is a powerful reality. This is the domain of Satan, and he doesn't want his favorite destructive myth taken away. He has used it to hold power for a long time, many thousands of years.

A Fundamental Dynamism

For Teilhard, these two forces—activities and passivities—permeate every aspect of creation and life. In an evolutionary process, they may be contrasted as spirit trying to emerge from within matter (activities) and matter resisting (passivities of diminishment). At the human level of development, some might call activities the energies of creativity and passivities of diminishment the energies of entropy.

Human thought and freedom affect activities and passivities in new and surprising ways. For the first time in evolutionary history, nature and life can be controlled, or at least managed, by human thought. Thus, evolution itself can now be consciously piloted, activities can be planned and modified for better effectiveness, and the diminishments that flow from passitivities can be transcended and turned into growth. The creative mind can find ways to overcome entropy. The grace to do so is always present and ready in the divine milieu. Working with the power of the divine spirit and divine creativity, almost every diminishment can be transformed into growth for the Christ Body.

The same grace is available to groups and organizations when the group's mind, heart, and spirit are integrated and they share a self-transcending purpose that can further the work of the Christ Project.

Jesus recognizes and teaches that people under the domination system and the myth of redemptive violence can change their direction. And the destructive system and myth can be changed for one of redemptive love. To teach us this truth is his mission, and what he models for us.

The Christ Project, this vision of the fullness of the kingdom of God, reflects a daring optimism that believes in the ultimate success of God's plan. Because of God's grace, our belief in the ultimate success of the Christ Project utterly transforms our approach to sin and temptation. Sin and temptation are turned into challenges to be overcome, not dwelt on and lamented, but events to be acknowledged and transcended by divine grace. Even the omnipresent and seemingly insurmountable domination system can be redeemed, not by violence but by love and compassion. Love and compassion represent the irresistible power of God's grace flowing through the human spirit. Domination's myth of redemptive violence can be rejected, replaced, and transcended, which is what Jesus does in his temptations in the desert.

In each temptation, Satan commands Jesus, in effect, "Do what I tell you." And Jesus replies, "I will not do what you want but what God wants me to do."

The Temptations of Jesus: Meditation (Matthew 4:1–11; Basic Principle 15)

First Prelude: Here it will be to acknowledge the fact that, while the Holy Spirit is energizing the universal Body of Christ toward its evolutionary fulfillment, there are also devolutionary forces holding back that Body's progress, such as the domination system and its belief that peace and justice can best be achieved through violence. We all are affected by many worldwide "passivities of diminishment," as Teilhard calls them.

Personally, our diminishments include not only the destructive social systems that weaken us and keep us from being all that we can be, but more often the harmful elements of the "givens" of our personal life. These diminishments that burden us, that are not of our own making, may include, for example, being born in an abusive household or in a country riddled with terrorism, being abandoned as a child, physical weakness or chronically poor health, our materialist culture, an overly-demanding profession, unsatisfactory relationships, negative experiences with institutional religion, etc. All of these have their own power to weaken us and tempt us away from what we can do for Christ. The focus of this meditation is to find and clarify the root sources of our own temptations to devolve rather than evolve.

Second Prelude: Here perhaps you can sit on the sidelines and watch Jesus as he encounters these temptations to lure him away from his mission and commitment, to see how he deals with them. Or you can dialogue with Jesus to find out the process that goes on in his mind and spirit as he deals with each temptation. What you discover in your dialogue may also be personally helpful to you.

Third Prelude: Here it will be to ask for the grace to recognize the temptations that would lure you away from the mission God has entrusted to you—in the physical, psychological, and spiritual domains—and to discover their sources. You may ask for the grace to recognize your most vulnerable places. You may also ask for the grace to recognize temptations to abandon or avoid the work you are called to do to further the Christ Project. Ask to recognize temptations even before they become strong or almost irresistible, and for the grace to resist them. Always pray for the grace to be able personally to contribute to the growth and development of the Body of Christ.

1. TEMPTATIONS IN THE PHYSICAL DOMAIN

Observe Jesus as he confronts his first temptation to detour from his mission—to turn stones into bread—and dialogue with him to find out how he deals with it. Ask him about your vulnerability to temptation in the physical domain. Ask him to point out those pockets of weakness and diminishment in your physical life that you may not recall. Ask Jesus how his example might help, guide, and advise you to deal with them, especially as they might distract you from your mission.

Note: In general, this first temptation relates to all temptations that have to do with the physical domain. Here, you may consider whether temptations toward excessive eating or drinking, or to laziness and uncooperativeness, might be your excuse to say no to God. You may be among those who are regularly tempted to anger, resentment, revenge, violence, or other forms of abuse, physical and sexual. Notice that none of the temptations Jesus faced was of a sexual or violent nature, while people today are constantly faced with temptations to violence as well as to sexual violations and relational infidelity. We live in an age and culture where violence and sexual excess are often accepted, condoned, and sometimes approved.

It is useful to note that the opposites of these temptations in the physical realm are also very common today. Instead of violence toward others, we see in people today forms of violence toward self: physical self-abuse such as extreme nutritional restriction that may lead to anorexia or bingeing that may lead to bulimia. In this context also today, we commonly observe temptations to addictions to alcohol, drugs, spending, gambling, pornography, using people for our own selfish satisfaction, and the like. None of these were Jesus' temptations, but they are very prevalent today.

Neither was Jesus tempted to think of his body as shameful or that something was wrong with him, that his body was a source of sin, or that his appearance was not attractive. These are very common self-focused temptations today that keep people from loving and serving God's plans for them.

2. Temptations in the Psychological Domain

Observe Jesus as he confronts his second subtle temptation to jump from the pinnacle of the temple. It was a temptation to impress others rather than stay focused on what God asks of him. Dialogue with Jesus to find out how he deals with it. Ask him about your vulnerability to temptation in the psychological and emotional domains. Reflect with him on how you have dealt with them in the past regarding your ability to stay focused on what God asks of you, and what you might wish to do differently from now on.

Note: In general, this second temptation connects to all temptations that have to do with the mental and emotional domains as well as those that are ego related. Here, you may consider temptations to greed, power, jealousy, envy, and entitlement, all of which permeates the domination system. They are powerful distractions from the work of the Christ Project, and very prevalent temptations today.

Then, there are the opposites of these, including temptations to self-depreciation and putting down, denying or ignoring one's abilities and talents. Such poor self-respect and self-esteem could lead to the belief that I am of no value and have nothing to offer. Other psychological temptations may include believing that I am stupid, unlovable, unloving, and that I have no power to make a difference anywhere. You may also be tempted to use as an excuse to avoid God's work the claim that "I was once deeply wounded and hurt by the cruel words and actions of someone, and I will never recover from that wound."

Fear is also a major temptation in our day. Fear lies at the root of our preoccupation with keeping safe and secure. Fear keeps people from taking action. It also leads people to convince themselves that they cannot make a difference, so why even try.

3. Temptations in the Spiritual Domain

Observe Jesus as he confronts his third temptation, to boldly worship Satan and commit to the domination system. Dialogue with him to find out how he deals with it. Ask him about your vulnerability to temptation in the spiritual domain, your need for courage, commitment, and determination to carry out your mission. Ask him how you can notice temptations coming before they occur. Talk about how you have dealt with them or given in to them, and why.

Note: In general, this third temptation relates to all temptations that focus on the spiritual domain, especially pride, entitlement, a sense of superiority, and presumption—or their opposites, such as despair, hopelessness, bitterness, and loss of faith. One wise person when told that pride was the root of all sin replied, "Perhaps not pride, but ingratitude is the deepest root of all."

Colloquy: Ask for help in combating your temptations and for the grace to keep your work for and awareness of Christ primary in your life.

Review: Conduct a review as usual. You may have received insights about your vulnerabilities during this prayer time, insights you will want to take to heart as you continue to make the Exercises. Be sure to make note of these.

Call of the Seventy-two Disciples: Meditation (Luke 10:10–24; Basic Principle 10)

First Prelude: Imagine the scene as Jesus pairs his many disciples and sends them forth on their first mission.

Second Prelude: Ask for the grace to commit yourself to the service of others for the sake of Christ and the Christ Project. Ask to learn some secrets of ministry from this story.

The following are some suggestions of facts to explore during your prayer time.

- Jesus does not choose only a special few but sends out all of the disciples who are present that day—at least seventy of them. Today, too, he is calling everyone to build the Body of Christ, not just clergy and vowed religious.
- Jesus does not send his disciples out alone, but with a partner for support, companionship, encouragement, and sharing. The kingdom of God, then and today, involves working in small teams.
- When Jesus says, "Carry no purse, no bag, no sandals; and greet no one on the road," he is saying to us that you (just yourself and not your belongings) are both the messenger and the message. (Note: In Hebrew tradition, "greeting" someone on the road called for a rather involved and time-consuming formal ritual requiring shared meals and storytelling. It did not involve merely a passing word and a wave of the hand, as it might today.)
- The small teams are to go to places where Jesus has not yet gone to announce the good news.
- The first gift they are to offer when they come to a new place is the gift of peace.
- They are to be sensitive whether or not their peace is accepted, and stay or leave accordingly. It is perhaps too

difficult to announce good news to those who are not even open to peace and tranquility.

- Once disciples are accepted in a certain place, they are not to move about, but to stay and carry out their mission in that place.
- They are not to demand any privileges or special requirements for themselves, but quietly, as guests, accept the room and board that is offered.
- The second gift they are to offer is healing.
- The third gift is to announce to the people in that village, "the kingdom of God is near to you."
- Even if the disciples are unwelcome and can do nothing else, they are to announce the presence of the kingdom of God, even as they leave a place.
- This announcement is the proclamation of the presence of the Christ Body. "Whoever listens to you listens to me, and whoever rejects you rejects me, and whoever rejects me rejects the one who sent me."
- "I have given you authority to tread on snakes and scorpions, and over all the power of the enemy; and nothing will hurt you." This is the guarantee that ultimately your soul will not be harmed.
- The call to service will bring you joy: "The seventy returned with joy...."
- The call to serve the Christ Project is something even children can understand. "I thank you, Father, Lord of heaven and earth, because you have hidden these things from the wise and the intelligent and have revealed them to infants; yes, Father, for such was your gracious will."
- The final victory is assured. "All things have been handed over to me by my Father; and no one knows who the Son is except the Father, or who the Father is except the Son and anyone to whom the Son chooses to reveal him."

Colloquy: Express your gratitude to Jesus for his insights about how to be a disciple.

Parables of the Kingdom

Some Assumptions

Assumption 1: Whenever Jesus is describing what he calls the kingdom of God or the kingdom of heaven, it is more than a description of the afterlife or life in heaven. In most kingdom parables there is always some activity, human responsibility, choices made, or a change of heart, all of which suggests that the kingdom is something happening here on Earth, a divine project that is in process here and now, something ongoing, something big. From an evolutionary standpoint, whenever you see the expression "kingdom of God," you may read "Christ Project."

Assumption 2: Parables are not conceptual statements; they are metaphorical stories. They are not factual but point to important insights or meanings. They are more like poetry than prose, more like a song's melody than its lyrics, more like dancing than walking. As stories of human experience, parables have many levels of meaning.

The kingdom—or the Christ Project, for us—cannot be captured in declarative sentences. It must be experienced, felt, sensed, perceived; understood rather than defined; intuited rather than conceptualized. The mode of explanation Jesus used to talk about the kingdom was the parable. A parable is a piece of art meant to be experienced, tasted, mulled over, and pondered—something to meditate on, not simply to be explained.

Note: It is true that in the gospel texts Jesus is sometimes portrayed as calling his special disciples aside and giving a single interpretation of a parable to them, as in the case of the farmer who went out to sow the seed. While the interpretation put into the mouth of Jesus by the gospel writers can certainly be one valid interpretation, there may be many more ways of viewing this parable. Perhaps the gospel writers felt it necessary to present a specific interpretation in the text, or perhaps the explanation in the text happened to be the one that teachers in the early church were accustomed to using. And the gospel writers realized the interpretation would have much more power if it were put into the mouth of Jesus.

Assumption 3: In his descriptions of the kingdom of God, Jesus uses what is called *both/and thinking*. For him, the kingdom cannot be encapsulated in words—it is not *this* or *that*. Rather, it is like a mustard seed, yeast, a hidden treasure, a merchant searching, a fishnet, a storehouse, etc. No one of these images completely captures the nature of the kingdom; all of them and many more are needed to begin to comprehend what this great project is. Understanding the kingdom—or the Christ Project—requires both/and thinking.

Both/and thinking is in contrast to *either/or thinking*, which is the primary way we have been trained to think in our culture. We would tend to ask, "Is the kingdom of God either this or that? Is it more like a mustard seed or is it more like yeast? Seeds and yeast are very different, so it can't be both." Either/or thinking emphasizes differences, distinctions. It is very logical and linear. It is exclusive. Either/or thinking is not helpful in this context, where Jesus is using both/and thinking. The kingdom is not either this or that, it is like *both* this *and* that. Each image merely highlights a different aspect or quality of the kingdom of God (or the Body of Christ).

Note: Sometimes, because the gospel writers were, like us, conditioned to be either/or thinkers, they tended to reshape Jesus' both/and thinking into their own either/or mentality. They would try to reduce what was very complex into something very simple and logical. That may be their cultural limitation. Don't make it yours.

Assumption 4. In Jesus' time, there was no concept of evolution, as we know it today. Their closest approach to the idea of evolution is found in words like *growth* or *development*. Some of Jesus' images for the kingdom emphasize things that grow and develop organically, like a bush emerging from a seed, or yeast gradually permeating all the elements of the bread dough. Neither of these images implies a numerical growth but rather emphasizes a kind of organic development or an evolving process.

As you go through this meditation, try not to be caught up in traditional either/or thinking. Do not get hooked by seeing the kingdom as something exclusively defined by its numerical increase.

Parables of the Kingdom: Meditation (Matthew 13:31–35, 47–48; Basic Principles 2 and 3)

First Prelude: Imagine the Creator envisioning a great evolutionary plan for creation, setting it in motion guided by the law of love, watching it come to a level of consciousness where it is ready to receive revelation of the Creator's plan, and assigning the divine Son, Jesus, with the task of introducing people to this great work.

Second Prelude: Imagine Christ, in his own prayer and thoughts, struggling to find ways to explain the Creator's great project to his followers, and how he chooses various images of the kingdom of God or the kingdom of heaven to use for this purpose.

Third Prelude: Ask for the grace to find in the kingdom parables a deeper understanding of the nature of what God has planned for us, and the ways Jesus uses both/and thinking to counteract the limiting, either/or ways of thinking so prevalent among his followers. Ask also for the grace to know what Jesus is saying that "has been hidden from the foundation of the world."

1. Consider the first of the images Jesus uses to describe the nature of the kingdom of God (or the Creator's Christ Project). Notice the evolutionary or process emphasis in the mustard seed and the yeast. Apply this insight to what is happening in the world today, and talk to Jesus about what it might mean for the process of the evolving Christ Body. In the parable of the mustard seed, what might the birds symbolize today? In the parable of the yeast, what might the woman symbolize today? What things today could the flour represent in God's plan?

He put before them another parable: "The kingdom of heaven is like a mustard seed that someone took and sowed in his field; it is the smallest of all the seeds, but when it has grown it is the greatest of shrubs and becomes a tree, so that the birds of the air come and make nests in its branches" (Matt 13:31–32).

He told them another parable: "The kingdom of heaven is like yeast that a woman took and mixed in with three measures of flour until all of it was leavened" (Matt 13:33).

Jesus told the crowds all these things in parables; without a parable he told them nothing. This was to fulfill what had been spoken through the prophet: "I will open my mouth to speak in parables; I will proclaim what has been hidden from the foundation of the world" (Matt 13:34–35).

2. Ask Jesus what he is trying to reveal in these next two images—the hidden treasure and the searching merchant—especially to people today, and reflect on how these two images relate to the evolutionary work that lies before us. Both parables emphasize the idea of discovery, the discovery of what I am meant to do in my life and what is most spiritually valuable for me.

The kingdom of heaven is like treasure hidden in a field, which someone found and hid; then in his joy he goes and sells all that he has and buys that field (Matt 13:44).

Again, the kingdom of heaven is like a merchant searching for fine pearls; on finding one pearl of great value, he went and sold all that he had and bought it (Matt 13:45–46).

Commentary: Notice that in the hidden treasure parable, Jesus is not saying that there is only one field, or that only one person will find the treasure and that everyone else will be left out. That is either/or thinking; the other images of the kingdom assure us that this is not a proper interpretation of the parable. The treasure image may have many implications, but exclusivity of salvation is not one of them. More likely, the uniqueness of your individual contribution to the building up of the Body of Christ is one meaning of them. Ask yourself, "Why does the person buy the whole field?" and "What might the whole field symbolize?"

In the second parable of the pair, many people immediately assume that Jesus' focus is on the "pearl of great value." If you read it carefully, you will see that here Jesus is not emphasizing the pearls. He is not saying that the kingdom of heaven is like a pearl of great value, but rather that the kingdom of heaven is like a *merchant searching*. If you were a merchant searching, what would that feel like? If Christ—or the evolving Body of Christ—were the merchant searching, what might he be searching for?

3. The net, especially a fishermen's net, is a sort of catchall. It collects things indiscriminately. It gathers everything in its path. It misses nothing. Only later are the contents of the net sorted out. As you think of the evolving Body of Christ, what kinds of things could the net symbolize? What might the shore symbolize? Who might the fishermen symbolize? Why would they sit down to do the sorting work?

Again, the kingdom of heaven is like a net that was thrown into the sea and caught fish of every kind; when it was full, they drew it ashore, sat down, and put the good into baskets but threw out the bad (Matt 13:47–48).

Commentary: The either/or interpretation of this fishnet parable that Matthew puts into the mouth of Jesus (Matt 13:49–50) limits the richness and power of the image. Besides, Jesus seldom "interprets" the meaning of the parable when speaking to the crowd as he is doing here.

Note that Jesus does not say that what was saved or thrown out are individual fish (or individual persons). He is not specific in this regard. We know that he would want everyone to be saved. So then, what could the net represent? Who might the fishermen be? What would it mean to "throw out" the bad?

What might the parable suggest if what was caught in the net represented all of the different parts of a single person?

4. As you come to understand the meaning and symbolism of the kingdom parables, you are being trained to be a "master" for the kingdom. You are filling up your mental and spiritual storehouse for helping build the Body of Christ, so that when you meet others who want to understand the Christ Project, you have a storehouse full of ideas and ways to promote the work of the kingdom. Some of these ideas are new, others are older. During your interactions with others, you will know best when to bring out new ideas from your storehouse and when to bring out old ones.

"Have you understood all this?" They answered, "Yes." And he said to them, "Therefore every scribe who has been trained for the kingdom of heaven is like the master of a household who brings out of his storehouse what is new and what is old" (Matt 13:51–52).

Colloquy: Ask Jesus to remind you of your special role in helping build the Body of Christ. Ask him to remind you of the skills, talents, capacities, connections, friends, and opportunities you already have in your storehouse of things new and old. Ask that you learn to love the evolving Body of Christ and all the persons and things in it.

Reflection: In your journal, list some of the items, both new and old, that you have available in your storehouse. You may also recall times when you have used one or other of them to promote the development of the Body of Christ.

The Woman Who Was a Sinner

Although Jesus of Nazareth never gave us anything like Teilhard's law that drives the evolution of the Body of Christ—the Law of Attraction-Connection-Complexity-Consciousness—Jesus is a model practitioner. Although the Christ that is alive today is the Cosmic Christ, we still turn to his Earth-life example, since he is the one human who knew the Father's plan for humanity. He is also a model of evolutionary behavior, even though he would have never described himself in those terms.

If the Father's plan had been merely to save individual human souls, bring them to heaven and let the Earth and all creation disappear, Jesus would probably not have spent so much effort confronting and trying to change unjust human structures in society. He would more likely have encouraged people simply to "flee the world" and think about nothing but God. Instead, during his life on Earth, Jesus was consciously keeping that evolutionary process in motion.

As long as the Body of Christ on Earth is still developing and maturing, it will have to stay healthy, nourish itself with love, and heal its infections and wounds. This is our task today. To use all our resources of wisdom, knowledge, science, technology, psychology, sociology, anthropology, ecology, and so on, to keep the Christ Body healthy, nourish it, and heal it as best we can.

From the stories we have about how Jesus relates to people, we learn how Jesus works to build up consciousness in the Body of Christ. We observe him so we can imitate his methods and live his values. Watch how he interacts differently with each character.

The Woman Who Was a Sinner: Meditation (Luke 7:36–50; Basic Principle 3)

First Prelude: The Creator loves Jesus ("This is my beloved Son in whom I am well pleased.") as he proclaims the message of the divine "standard" and struggles to make people understand what God is calling humanity to become.

Second Prelude: Here see Jesus reclining at table in Simon the Pharisee's home, surrounded by Simon's friends, when a woman comes in, kneels at Jesus' feet, and begins to weep. Use your imagination with all its sensory powers to place yourself in the scene, perhaps as a guest at table, or as a servant, or as an unnoticed observer.

Third Prelude: Here ask for the graces you need, namely, to have the wisdom of Jesus when dealing with each kind of person you encounter so that you are loving and forgiving to those who need this, and tactfully kind yet clever to those who need a different response.

1. JESUS AND THE WOMAN

You may watch Jesus' interactions with the woman in the story. Notice how he uses the Law of Attraction-Connection-Complexity-Consciousness.

Interact contemplatively with Jesus and with the woman. Dialogue with them. Ask each of them questions that might clarify how and why they respond the way they do. Ask questions out of curiosity. For example, you might ask Jesus how he is using the loving evolutionary forces of attraction and connection with her.

You might ask the woman how she had come to know Jesus, how she knew he could forgive her "sin," and how she managed to get inside Simon's house. Ask also how she responded to the way Jesus treated her, and how it changed her life. Become her confidant. Ask her about the alabaster jar of ointment she brings and its significance to her; that may be a story in itself.

Commentary: Notice that Luke does not name the woman's sin or sins, other than implying that every one of Simon's dinner guests knew of her. While many have traditionally assumed she was a prostitute, this is by no means necessarily true. There are other possible examples of her sin. She may have publicly left her husband or children; she may be living with a man who is not her husband; she may be the town gossip and publicly slanders people; she may have had a child out of wedlock; she may have a mental illness like schizophrenia or be physically disfigured; she may be someone who blatantly defies religious customs and hence is "unclean." Any of these could be her sin. You may ask her about the choices that generated in her such deep sorrow and enough tears to wash someone's feet. In your dialogue, she may ask you if you have ever committed sin that released such sorrow.

As for Jesus' behavior, he doesn't stop the woman from touching him, an act that would automatically make Jesus ritually unclean ("sinful"). He says nothing to her during the entire process, until the very end. Without talking, he seems to know what she needs, and he provides it. Jesus is always nurturing the kingdom; he is always trying to bring people to a higher level of consciousness.

He is the way, the one who is your model.

Note: Please record in your journal your questions and the responses that you hear in your soul from Jesus and the woman. The woman will teach you what people like her need. Jesus will teach you how best to be of service to such people.

If you use up your entire meditation period with just this first point, that is all right. But be sure to have a colloquy with Jesus or the Creator before you end your prayer time. You may come back to the other points later in the day or at another time.

2. JESUS AND SIMON THE PHARISEE

You may watch Jesus' interactions with Simon. Notice how differently Jesus uses the Law of Attraction-Connection-Complexity-Consciousness in this encounter, especially as he builds complexity and consciousness in Simon's mind.

Dialogue with each of them, if you wish. Ask each of them questions that might clarify their interaction. For example, you might ask Jesus how he is using the loving evolutionary forces of complexity and consciousness with Simon. Ask Jesus what he hoped to accomplish with Simon during this opportunity.

Ask probing questions of Simon, too. Ask him what he really thinks of Jesus. Ask about his feelings during the woman's scene and in his subsequent exchange with Jesus. Ask if he changed in his attitude toward Jesus after this event, or did he just become more fixed in his wish to trick or demean Jesus in front of his friends.

Commentary: Notice that, like Jesus, Simon says nothing at the intrusive entrance of the woman, and nothing during the entire time she weeps. Why? Did he know ahead of time that the woman would try to barge into his home? Did he somehow "set up" her appearance just to test Jesus? Had he planned this "show" in advance to entertain his friends? Why did he say and do nothing all this time?

We know that in Israel at that time, it was customary for a host to provide three welcoming courtesies when a guest came to visit and dine. First you would see that your guest's feet were rinsed of the dust from the road; second, that they were dried with a towel; and third, rubbed with oil or lotion to preserve moisture in the skin. Jesus points out to Simon his neglect, not as a criticism or complaint, but as a simple fact and in contrast to the behavior of the woman. Jesus is thereby creating "complexity" in Simon's mind by forcing him to observe the difference between his and her paradoxical welcoming behavior, as a preparation to stretch Simon's consciousness.

You will also notice that Jesus gives Simon three opportunities for a change of heart. First, he accepts Simon's invitation to dinner even though he knows Simon is planning to mistreat him (Jesus forgives him in advance). Second, he lets Simon watch someone (the woman) who seeks forgiveness and undergoes a change of heart (Jesus presents an example for Simon to observe). Third, Jesus poses a question in the simple parable about the master forgiving the debts of two servants who could not repay what they owed. Simon gives the correct answer, but doesn't realize that he might be the one who owes his master the greater debt; he doesn't even realize he is in debt. Throughout all this, notice that Jesus never condemns Simon.

3. Jesus and the Other Guests

Luke mentions nothing about the other guests (there would be only men) seated around Simon's table, yet we know they were there and witnessed the woman's appearance and actions. Like Simon, none of them said or did anything while the woman washed and dried Jesus' feet.

In a contemplative dialogue, perhaps you might take two or three men aside, one by one, and dialogue with each one of them separately. Do not rush the process. Dialogue in private. Ask each one about his relationship to Simon and how he came to be invited to this dinner. Was he a business partner? Did Simon owe him a favor?

Ask each one why he didn't speak up when the woman came in? Was he afraid of offending Simon? Did he come to the dinner hoping for a "show"? Did he feel superior to Jesus and the woman? Did he have any kind of change of heart toward Jesus or toward the woman? Ask him what he thinks it would have taken to get him and the other guests to change their hearts?

Notice that, in your dialogues, not all of the guests will give you the same answer to each question. Some will be cynics. Others will be sycophants. Others will be bored and looking for a diversion. A few may be genuine seekers.

After each dialogue, you may turn to Jesus and ask him how you could interact with each type of bystander in order to make a connection, build complexity into the dialogue, and hopefully raise consciousness. Jesus may ask you how you would have responded had you been a guest at this dinner.

Note: As before, you may use the written dialogue prayer technique to record your interactions.

Commentary: There are many kinds of bystanders in the kingdom. Some stand by and do nothing out of fear. Some relish the defeat of goodness. Some are fixed in their sense of superiority. Some criticize. Some blame. Some play helpless. Perhaps you can imagine that each of the guests at the table is a different kind of bystander. Choose which two or three of these to dialogue with.

Note: Please record in your journal your questions and the responses that you hear in your soul from each guest. Each man will teach you what people like him require in order to have a change of heart; Jesus will teach you how best to be of service to—or challenge—such people.

Colloquy: Tell Jesus reverently what you learned during this contemplation about being an evolutionary disciple, and about how to use the Law of Attraction-Connection-Complexity-Consciousness in your daily encounters with people. Renew your commitment to serve Christ in his work. Ask for the graces you need to be courageous and not to be a bystander in so important a project. Ask for the graces to be patient, forgiving, and noncondemning, and to use wise action.

A Different Kind of Fire

Jesus said to his disciples: "I came to bring fire to the earth, and how I wish it were already kindled! I have a baptism with which to be baptized, and what stress I am under until it is completed!" (Luke 12:49–50).

Fire is a symbol of passionate commitment. It is the kind of holy fire and commitment we desire to feel in our hearts in order to move from the second to the Third Week of the Exercises. From the fire of Jesus' love flows the eagerness[8] for his new baptism. Jesus almost cannot wait for this new baptism to happen (Basic Principles 12 and 14).

A few years before, Jesus had received the baptism of John in the Jordan River. So, what is this new baptism that Jesus, now in the middle of his public life, is being called to undergo? Traditionally, most scripture scholars interpret this new "baptism" as Jesus' suffering, death, and resurrection. And indeed, it is a most legitimate interpretation.

However, it is important to remember the larger symbolic meaning or purpose of any kind of baptism. It represents a dying to something old and a being born to something new—going from an old life to a new life, a *metanoia*.

What if we were to re-envision this new baptismal desire of Jesus during his public life in an evolutionary way as Saint Paul does? He suggests that we think of Christ in his resurrection emerging as the new Adam, the beginning of a new species of human (1 Cor 15:22). We would then imagine Jesus in this experience coming to the realization that he has been destined from all eternity to be the new Cosmic Adam in which everything lives and moves and has its being. He is to be reborn or transformed into something entirely new.

Perhaps, from now on in his public life Jesus becomes emotionally preoccupied with this larger cosmic transformation, as if he in his human body is bound or constrained somehow, and needs to

8. The Greek verb here is *sunechomai*, which literally means "I am greatly anguished until [this baptism] is accomplished" or "I am emotionally constrained until…" or "I am totally preoccupied with it until…" or "I am under a compelling pressure until…."

be set free to become who he was meant to be from all eternity—the Person who holds all creation together.

He is on fire to have that transformation come about, even though he knows it may require his suffering and death. He is also aware that this great transformation may never fully happen during his time on Earth. But he knows that at least he will have started the process with his fire and his love.

Teilhard, too, connects the image of fire with love in an evolutionary prayer. "Someday, after mastering the winds, the waves, the tides and gravity, we shall harness for God the energies of love, and then, for a second time in the history of the world, man will have discovered fire."

For Teilhard, Jesus' task—his evolutionary, long-range challenge—is to make that cosmic awareness happen in each of us, making us conscious that we are all members, or cells, of his body. Awareness of this glorious transformation has already happened in Jesus, but it has yet to become a conscious awareness in a critical number of human beings. Jesus' new baptism, then, perhaps represents the start of his effort to bring about that "tipping point" of the evolutionary scales, that moment when most of the humans on our planet will have made this "second discovery of fire."

Even after many centuries, Christ has yet to set "fire" to all the Earth. His cosmic baptism is still happening in us and among us. One by one, we are being transformed. It is a process still in evolution.

Teilhard invites you to focus on Christ's fire of passionate commitment and seek to become enflamed with that same desire. He ardently desires that all humans come to realize that they are members of one Divine Body. Let this become the fire that consumes us, not merely that "I" be saved, but that the entire universal body of Christ comes to its complete fulfillment.

Setting the Earth on Fire: Meditation (Basic Principle 14)

First Prelude: Imagine the scene in Jesus' public ministry. Perhaps it is evening after all the crowds have dispersed. Jesus has come back from a period of private prayer and is speaking with his disciples, revealing to them what he has just learned about himself during prayer with his Father. He says: "I came to bring fire to the earth, and how I wish it were already kindled! I have a baptism with which to be baptized, and what stress I am under until it is completed!" (Luke 12:49–50).

Second Prelude: Imagine you step up to the Lord and ask him for the grace to experience his fire of passionate commitment, and to feel in yourself such great love for God and for creation that you too would want to set the world on fire.

Part One: Those Already on Fire

1. See with the eyes of your imagination, across the breadth of Earth, tens of thousands of men and women, who may seem like ordinary people but who are on fire, if not consciously for Christ yet very clearly for his desires, and who are committed to promoting evolutionary growth in a thousand different ways, depending on each one's particular talents and opportunities.

2. With the ears of your imagination, hear these men and women speaking to each other about how they have been transformed by a kind of baptism into this new awareness and enthusiasm. Hear how these people, each in his or her own unique ways, plan to use their resources, talents, and skills to work for the unity of all creation.

3. With your human spirit, breathe in the beautiful aroma of the enthusiasm of all these people and of the fire in their hearts for the great evolutionary project of the Creator. Notice how they exude a kind of contagious energy and optimism.

Part Two: Your Own Fire

1. With your imagination's *sense of taste*, taste the ordinary food that keeps you alive and nourishes your physical and emotional strength to do the holy work of a member of the great Body that lives in the divine milieu. Food keeps you vital and alive to do the work you are called to do.

2. With your imagination's *sense of touch*, hold each of the tools of your daily life and work, and realize that each one is an

instrument with which you can make your unique contribution to building the Earth, which is part of the Body of
Christ.

3. Notice how the *energy and optimism of others* who are in the
Body of Christ have touched you. Where in your body can
you feel their influence? How does their energy affect your
mind? How does it affect what you want to do or wish you
could begin doing to make a positive difference in the
world?

Colloquy: Speaking to Christ, however you prefer to experience his presence, talk to him about the persons you have known
who have worked—or are still working—with passionate commitment in this evolutionary cause. Give him thanks for all these inspiring examples and ask their help to realize the many opportunities
you have in your life to be like them. You may also acknowledge
some of the times you have failed to use opportunities for Christ.
More importantly, promise to use such opportunities well in the
future. Ask again for the grace to feel in your own heart the fire that
Christ felt, and to be fully aware of it so that you may be consciously
transformed from an individual human being into a member of the
Body of Christ. End with an Our Father.

Discernment and Decisions (Basic Principles 7 and 16)

Ignatius designed his Spiritual Exercises so that discernment and decisions would be central to the process. Originally, individuals typically made the Exercises seeking clarity in making a major life decision. Today people make the Exercises for many different reasons and for a variety of specific purposes or aims.

Ignatius offered those making his Exercises a number of ways, still very useful, to help discern how to carry out a desired purpose or to find help making a life-changing decision. He called the process "Making an Election" (see sections 169 through 189).

Since Ignatius' day, we have enriched our knowledge from psychology and neurology about how humans make decisions and what motivates them. In the New Spiritual Exercises, discernment and decisions are still central, except we now have some scientific knowledge to enrich and clarify the Ignatian process.

What you may hope to discern during these Spiritual Exercises is a glimpse of what God wants from you, that is, what God would like you to do with your life, what you may call your *destiny*. If you already feel quite certain of your destiny, then these Exercises may help confirm it, renew it, and perhaps even specify it more clearly for the near future.

Five Levels of Motivation for Making Choices

One of the evolutionary gifts we humans have inherited from our animal ancestors is a number of brains. More precisely, our one complex brain has many parts or subsections, each of which has different functions or responsibilities.

The oldest and most primitive part is the *brain stem*, also called the reptilian brain; it is common to all animals, even the most primitive reptiles and birds.

Next, we have also inherited a brain from our animal ancestors that is referred to as the *limbic system*; it sits atop our brain stem and is surrounded by the cerebral cortex.

The *cortex*, which fills the rest of your skull, has two hemispheres, the right and left. Each hemisphere has a dominant set of functions.

Each of these brains has its own special logic, its own ways of measuring, and its own ways of responding to input. Each part has its own motivation for making choices.

Sometimes different parts of the brain work at cross-purposes. Ideally, all the parts should work together as an integrated system.

All of these parts are interactive and each will want to participate in your discernment and decision-making. Ideally, each part will help confirm and define your discernment process and your decision.

Schematically, the brain system and its motivations may be diagrammed as something like this.

Brain part	Logic	Elements	Measure	Response/Tool
brain stem	kinesthetic	*sensations*	pleasure/pain	*approach/avoidance*
limbic system	limbic	*perceptions*	survival	*fight/flight/freeze*
left cortex	conceptual (linear)	*concepts*	control of tangible	*language, reasoning*
right cortex	convergence (nonlinear)	*systems*	control of intangible	*systems thinking*
whole brain	destiny (beyond linear)	*life choices*	life purpose	*discernment*

KINESTHETIC LOGIC

The brain stem—the part we share with even the most primitive creatures—uses kinesthetic motivation in making decisions. Kinesthetic motivation may be described as a *logic of touch and movement*. It governs *movement toward* (approach or attraction toward pleasure) and *movement away from* (avoidance of or repulsion from pain).

The key elements in "choices" based solely on kinesthetic logic are *pleasure and pain sensations*. Animals—and we too—are *attracted* to pleasurable experiences such as eating, being touched, resting, movement, and action. Animals and we are likewise *repulsed* by painful experiences such as wounding, hunger, disgusting smells or images, being physically constrained, or being prevented from rest and sleep. We humans make many decisions daily based primarily on kinesthetic logic. Kinesthetic logic often suggests what to choose on a restaurant menu or strongly influences our choice of clothing, especially in the color and texture of materials.

Kinesthetic logic also utilizes a basic form of *memory*, what we today call "cellular memory," that inheres in our skin, muscle, and bone. We are strongly affected by its drive to seek pleasure and avoid pain, sometimes to our greater detriment, such as when the sex drive and its promise of pleasure cause some men and women to betray their spouses.

Sadly, when kinesthetic motivation rules the whole brain and subordinates all other brain parts to its logic, seeking pleasure becomes a person's main function, and thus when the brain stem is fully turned on, addictions often develop and get reinforced.

Nevertheless, the brain stem may give you some clues as to your destiny. The following exercise focuses on the brain stem.

SPIRITUAL EXERCISE:
SEEKING THE BRAIN STEM'S ADVICE

The brain stem's motivation is very simple. It is either attracted to something or repelled by it. It finds something pleasurable and enjoyable or unpleasurable and even painful. It either approaches a situation or wants to avoid it.

Say a prayer to have your brain stem give its best advice to your situation, that is, how to fulfill the purpose for which you are making the Exercises.

Then, in a kind of contemplative quiet, propose your choice or decision to your brain stem. Picture yourself making a certain choice and living in that choice, so the brain stem has a chance to respond. The pleasure or pain will be felt somewhere in your body. It will be an organically felt response.

Then quietly check. Where in your body do you feel a response? When you picture yourself working or carrying on in the context of your choice or purpose, do you feel joy and attraction? If not, what do you feel? Boredom? Annoyance? Resistance? Does your brain stem tell you to avoid the place, the situation, and the people there? Or does it make you feel happy and content there?

Afterward, write in your journal a record of what transpired during your reflections.

> If you are discerning a major decision between two choices (say two job offers), do this process separately for each option.
>
> If there seems to be no clarity of response from your brain stem, perhaps you can write out a prayerful dialogue between you and your brain stem, where you ask it very direct questions and solicit a clear response.

LIMBIC LOGIC

Limbic logic, your second form of making choices, is centered in the *limbic system*, the part of the brain system that is above the brain stem and surrounded by the cerebral cortex. Your limbic brain may have some wisdom to offer you with respect to your decision.

While the criterion of choice in kinesthetic logic is pleasure or pain, and its choice is either to approach or avoid a stimulus, the criterion of choice in limbic logic is *survival* (or avoiding serious injury, destruction, and death), and its choice is either to *fight or flee*—or *freeze*. Its motivation is to detect danger and protect you from serious harm.

While kinesthetic logic grasps and processes only sensory stimuli, limbic logic grasps *perceptions and emotions* and processes them by *association*, that is, by pairing them together and comparing them to certain memories stored in the limbic system. For example, when I walk into the produce department of a supermarket, I am reminded happily of my grandmother's vegetable garden. However, whenever I see a large dog, I am immediately fearful because I was bitten by a dog as a child. Thus, stimuli for the limbic system are *pairs of perceptions and emotions as they relate to the organism's safety and survival.*

Sadly, when the limbic brain takes over control of the whole brain system, it often creates an obsession with the person's safety and security. In the extreme, it may generate *compulsions* such as hand washing and nail biting, etc., or various *phobic fears* such as agoraphobia, claustrophobia, fear of heights, etc. Such behaviors and fears have most likely been formed, reinforced, and remembered at the kinesthetic and limbic levels. Religous scrupulosity is a good example of this.

Just as it is important that psychologists and other healthcare professionals be familiar with the dynamics of these different forms of logic in dealing with clients, it is important that persons making major life decisions be aware of how these different parts of the brain function and how they may affect personal decisions. For, just as one would hardly use conceptual logic to choose the flavor for one's ice cream cone (that decision is usually done by kinesthetic logic), so it is hardly useful to use kinesthetic or limbic logic to construct the proof of a scientific hypothesis.

SPIRITUAL EXERCISE:
SEEKING YOUR LIMBIC SYSTEM'S ADVICE

Your limbic system is concerned about your safety and your survival. It is all about detecting anything fearful and what to do in the face of fear. When your limbic system sees or recognizes something dangerous, it wants you to fight it and struggle with it or flee from it—or freeze (not do anything or "play dead") until it passes.

Ask your limbic system to recognize the dangers that may arise in connection with your purpose in making the Exercises. Ask it to present you with relevant images, emotions, and associations that it holds in your memory banks.

Perhaps the most fruitful way to interact with your limbic system is to dialogue with it. Ask it to show you the images and feelings it holds that relate to your choice or the situation that needs to be discerned. These limbic brain concerns may relate to your health or your emotions or to the people with whom you will be involved in your major choice.

When the context or situation becomes emotionally clear, ask your limbic system whether you should go forward and engage (fight) with your choice despite its dangers and your fears, or should you walk away (flee) from the choice and prefer to remain safe elsewhere. Or perhaps it suggests that you simply wait quietly (freeze), that now is not the time to make the choice facing you.

Afterward, write in your journal a record of what transpired. Report the details of the dialogue you held with your limbic system.

Also make notes that compare or contrast the responses of your brain stem and your limbic system.

LEFT HEMISPHERE LOGIC

The left hemisphere of your cortex (the part of your brain behind your left eye) deals in *concepts and language*. It is a third source of decision-making. If the brain stem is motivated to seek pleasure and avoid pain, and if the limbic system is motivated to keep you safe from danger and harm, the left hemisphere brain is motivated to find ways to *manage and control the tangible world* around you. To do this, it uses language and *linear reasoning*, what we normally refer to as logic.

The left hemisphere manipulates concepts and ideas in order to come up with solutions that help you take control of your physical world. It is also the major tool used in obtaining scientific knowledge.

For example, suppose you walk into your kitchen and notice water on the floor coming from under the sink. Your brain stem sees this situation as something very unpleasant and would want to deny it or avoid it. However, your limbic system would report a danger that needs to be dealt with. If your limbic system is overly fearful, you might feel like running away; if it is well balanced, it might call up a memory of when a leak happened before and remind you that you were able to fix it. Your left hemisphere might go through a logical reasoning process something like this: "That old pipe has come loose again. I fixed it with a wrench before. Let me quickly get a wrench and tighten the connection to stop the leak."

Your left hemisphere with its linear logic may be used to help clarify a choice or confirm a decision already made.

SPIRITUAL EXERCISE: SEEKING YOUR LEFT HEMISPHERE'S ADVICE

On a fresh page of your journal, make two columns by drawing a vertical line down the middle of the page. On the left top, write "Reasons For" and on the right top, "Reasons Against."

Consider a choice that you have come to the Exercises to help resolve. Then in the respective columns begin to list the reasons that favor that choice and the reasons for rejecting it.

If you are being offered two choices in your discernment process, both of which would be salutary choices (such as two good jobs or two good positions), use a separate page for each and do the entire "Reasons For" and "Reasons Against" process for each.

Many people might tell you that when you add up the pluses and minuses, God wants you to take the choice with the most pluses. This may or may not be the case. Adding pluses and minuses is only one more part of your brain contributing its wisdom (or opinion).

You could at least compare these responses to those you received from the brain stem and limbic system exercises.

RIGHT HEMISPHERE LOGIC

The right hemisphere of your cortex (the part of your brain behind your right eye) deals in *pictures and structures*. Its motivation is to see the whole picture. It can observe the interactions of the parts of a system and picture their effects within and outside the system. The left hemisphere uses *linear logic*, the right hemisphere uses a *non-linear* way of thinking, sometimes called *systems thinking*. While the left hemisphere is focused on controlling *tangible things*, the right hemisphere is much more at home dealing with and managing *intangible things* such as interactions among the parts of a system or interactions among people.

The right hemisphere of the cortex also has a *sense of the consequences*, near and far, of choices being made. For example, with regard to the leaky pipe under the sink, the right hemisphere might suggest that since this leak keeps happening repeatedly, it will probably keep happening, so it would be wise to call a plumber, get to the root of the problem, and fix it once and for all.

SPIRITUAL EXERCISE: SEEKING YOUR RIGHT HEMISPHERE'S ADVICE

Again, recall that you are seeking wisdom from this part of your brain regarding a certain decision.

Consider one or other of the choices facing you. Use your right hemisphere to picture the various effects of your choice. What will happen to your health and well-being if you make this choice? How will it affect your health five and ten years from now? How will it affect the people who are closest to you? What changes are likely to happen in the quality of relationships with them? What will you have accomplished five, then ten years from now because of this choice? *Make note of all these in your journal.*

Also ask how this choice would affect others in your life, your family, the organizations you belong to, and the planet itself—in the short run and the long run.

With this new information, you may review from your brain stem exercise what pleasures or pains this choice may bring you.

With this new information, you may review from your limbic system exercise the sense of fear or the sense of safety and protection this choice may bring you.

With this new information, you may review from your left hemisphere exercise the advantages and disadvantages this choice may bring you.

You may note what you have learned thus far about your decision. However, it is still not the full picture.

DESTINY LOGIC

Destiny logic uses all of the human brain and more. Its workings are neither linear nor nonlinear, but are best described as *beyond linear*. Destiny logic's primary work is to deal with one's *life choices*; these include major choices about career, marriage, basic priorities, and ultimate values. In destiny logic, the measure of one's choices is always one's *life purpose* or destiny, what one has been called to do in one's lifetime (by God or by the Universe). Does my choice fit in with my life purpose, or does it lead me away from it? The tool used to test one's choices against one's destiny is *discernment*.

A discernment tool is nothing like linear logic. There is no way that one can deduce one's destiny by using linear logic, or even systems thinking. Rather, it seems at our present level of human development that one's destiny is only gradually discovered or revealed. Unless one is attuned to the idea of destiny, one may never really discover it or become consciously aware of it. Sometimes, people seem to be simply dropped or pushed into their destiny without ever becoming aware. Some even go kicking and screaming into it.

Ignatius suggested a way to tap into destiny logic. He uses the measurement of *inner peace*. For example, he suggests that you can use his method if you are making the Exercises to discern and decide which of two desirable jobs is more in line with your destiny, assuming you can take either one job or the other but not both. Ignatius' method is very simple yet very subtle.

SPIRITUAL EXERCISE:
SEEKING YOUR WHOLE BRAIN'S ADVICE

Consider the first of your (two) choices. Tell yourself that you have chosen it—"This is the decision I have made!"—and agree to live for two or three days as if you had really made that first choice. During this time, you are to monitor your deepest feelings or inner movements. You are looking primarily for a deep inner peace.

During these days, make note in your journal and share with your retreat guide your experience of inner peace or lack of it.

As a clear break, after two or three days, let go of having made that first choice and spend one day free of decision making to clear your mind and spirit.

On the following day, consider your second choice and tell yourself that you have chosen it and agree to live for two or three days as if you had really made this choice. During this time, you are to monitor your deepest emotions. You are looking primarily for a deep inner peace.

During these days, make note in your journal and share with your retreat guide your experience of peace or lack of it.

If there is a clear distinction between the feelings of inner peace in the two situations, the choice that brought the greatest peace is clearly a push in the direction of your destiny—but only a push.

As a summary activity, you may want to collect the results of the wisdom you received from each of the five logics related to brain parts. Note any patterns. Ultimately, the final choice is up to you.

Once you make that choice, both you and God must work within that choice. Your choice has now become part of the given that both you and God must work with.

End of the Second Week

Journal Review

Before you begin the Third Week of the Exercises, it is important to gather and reflect upon the graces and insights of the Second Week. One of the best ways of doing this is to reflectively reread all the entries in your retreat journal, starting from the beginning.

- Set aside at least an hour for this grace-filled process.
- Begin with a prayer for guidance, asking that in the rereading of your journal you may not miss any insight or grace you received, especially in relation to your purpose in making the Exercises.
- As you reread your journal entries, underline things that strike you.
- On a fresh page of your journal, write "Second Week Journal Review" and begin listing on this page the insights and graces of the past Week that you noticed or underlined.
- Close the process with a colloquy of gratitude, perhaps one with Our Lady, another with Christ, and one with the Creator.

Note: If you are making the Exercises in a small group or team, it may be useful to share with your team members some of what you have written on your Second Week journal review pages.

The Third Week

Perspective

During the Second Week, retreatants begin to realize that there are still many dimensions of the Christ Project to consider.

During the Third Week, Ignatius asks us to see how Jesus on the cross identifies with wounded creation, and accepts the task of reparation, healing and transforming the damage we have been doing to ourselves and to our planet (Basic Principle 15).

Ignatius would say Jesus loves you so much that he wants to show that love by identifying with you as victim of your own sin. Jesus is also trying to make you conscious of the power of divine love to integrate your wounded goodness (and that of everyone else) into himself and, then, to move from a preoccupation with sin to a focus on grace (Eph 1:7–8).

Teilhard would add that Jesus identifies with your wounded goodness because he views you as an important part of his universal Body. He invites you to move beyond worrying about any of your inadequacies or failures in the past because he wants you to focus on what needs to be done in the future to complete God's project and your potential contribution to it (see Eph 1:9–10; 2 Cor 5:15). In addition to reparation, loving service is what Jesus was doing, even on the cross.

The Father has given Jesus an evolutionary mission, one that will require the cooperation, conscious or unconscious, of every generation of human beings until the end of time. Jesus has invited you to be consciously on his team in your generation to help carry forward his divine mission (Eph 1:4–6).

The Passion and Death of Jesus

One of Ignatius' hopes throughout the Spiritual Exercises is that the retreatant will learn to put on the mind and heart of Jesus, since he is the "way" to live (Basic Principle 9).

In Jesus' public life, which is the focus of the Second Week, he shows us how to be active and proactive (Eph 4:1–7).

In his passion, which is the focus of the Third Week, Jesus is showing us how to deal with the unwelcome and unavoidable passivities of our lives that we must endure, whether we like it or not. Jesus shows us how to turn these passivities into instruments of growth and evolution (Phil 1:29; Eph 4:5).

Jesus' Attitude toward Suffering

Jesus does not suffer or willingly undergo suffering merely for the sake of suffering. We have no example of Jesus during his life consciously and freely inflicting pain or suffering on himself as a form of prayer or devotion to God. Jesus did not approve of suffering for the sake of suffering.

Across the board, Jesus is not in favor of suffering, whether physical, mental, or emotional. Whenever he saw pain or suffering in those who came to him, he tried to heal it or relieve it, not prolong it or tell someone suffering was good for them. His healing miracles tell us that he relieved pain and suffering whenever possible. He relieved even the pangs of normal hunger in the feeding of the five thousand.

When it came to his own suffering during his passion, he approached it in the same way. What Jesus dealt with in his passion was *unavoidable suffering*, pain, and humiliation inflicted on him by others. His passion was a *passivity*, a series of physical and emotional diminishments; they were nothing he would have chosen or desired in themselves. We know from his prayer to his Father during the agony in the garden that, if it were possible, he would prefer not to have to go through with the suffering and his death (Luke 22:42). He endured what happened because of the choices and desires of others. His passion was the inevitable result of the process he was put through by the leaders of the temple and the Roman officials.

Jesus accepted the pain and humiliation of his trial, his scourging, his crowning, carrying the cross, and his crucifixion primarily because it was part of being faithful to his mission and destiny (Phil 2:6–11). Pain and humiliation are a normal and natural part of everyone's mission (Col 1:11–12).

However, because Jesus was motivated and driven by love and forgiveness, he turned his pain and suffering into a positive force. This is what Jesus asks us also to do.

If a woman wants to become a ballerina, she must undergo thousands of hours of grueling practice, much physical pain, and emotional frustration, with the consequent loss of social life and entertainment that others typically enjoy. All these are forms of unavoidable and inevitable diminishment that she willingly accepts as part of carrying out her positive mission to become a ballerina.

A pharmaceutical chemist searching for a cure for a certain disease may have to spend many long and sleepless hours of overtime in the laboratory doing his research, unable to leave an experiment until it is complete. He may make many attempts to find a cure and have little or no success, but only a string of failures to show for his efforts. These are unavoidable and inevitable diminishments of his physical and emotional life that he willingly accepts as part of carrying out his proactive commitment to find a cure.

However, enduring such trials—such as countless hours of disciplined practice or monotonous work in the laboratory—has another benefit. It provides an opportunity to grow in appreciation of things that are important in life—such as discovering who you truly are and are meant to be. We can hope that the ballerina and the chemist will enjoy such a discovery. In this sense, as Jesus endures the tribulations of his passion, he becomes more conscious of who he is and who he has been called by God to be.

With Consciousness and Love

Jesus was always ready to heal the pain and suffering of others. People today still pray that Jesus will relieve their suffering or heal their diseases. However, what often happens to these people of faith when their sufferings cannot be healed is that they endure with consciousness and love any diminishment these sufferings bring (2 Cor

1:5–7). We all know stories of people who endured unavoidable suffering and transformed it through consciousness and love. Any diminishment always provides an opportunity to grow in appreciation of things that are important in life (Gal 6:14).

As a woman on her deathbed expressed it, "I used to want to get an A in life. As I get closer to death, I become a faster and faster learner. As I lose my outer capacities—my beauty and use of my limbs—I become much more conscious of who I am in terms of my inner life and caring for others who are suffering. I am trying to develop my inner beauty and deep gratitude for life."

Humans are the bearers of consciousness and free choice. Thus, we can endure unavoidable suffering with consciousness and hatred, or we can endure it with consciousness and love. When you are conscious of your suffering, you can take the energy of your suffering and direct it either into anger and resentment, or into compassion and healing.

In his passion and death, Jesus teaches us how to suffer with consciousness and love. It is an important lesson and grace to learn from meditating on the passion. Teilhard also recognized this truth and wrote,

> What a leap forward the world would make toward God if all sick people at the same time converted their pain into a common desire that the reign of God should rapidly mature through the conquest and organization of the earth. All the sufferers on earth uniting their sufferings so that the world's pain became a great and unique act of consciousness—would that not be one of the highest forms which the mysterious work of creation could take in our eyes?

Until we can get beyond seeing nothing more on the cross than Jesus as an individual in excruciating agony, we can never grasp the conscious creative and redemptive force of his suffering and death. The evolutionary meaning of the passion will elude us. So, we ask for the grace to comprehend his passion and death as an action where the inexpressible intensity of his consciousness absorbs not only all the energy and intensity of his personal suffering but also that of all the sin, suffering, and pain of creation, past, present, and future. And he redirects it toward the goal of the mission given him by the Father.

Teilhard points out a fact that many people miss, namely, that suffering requires a tremendous output of energy, and that this energy exists in the divine milieu. Jesus was victimized but he never became a helpless victim. Instead, Jesus redirected this suffering-energy during his passion toward service for others (Rom 5:21). He did this consciously while on the cross, which is clear from his words: compassion for the thief, forgiveness of his enemies, and care for his mother. Even in those moments of unendurable pain, he never forgot his redemptive mission of reparation, forgiveness, and healing.

Redirecting his own suffering-energy is exactly what Saint Paul did with the pain and hurt he endured. "I am now rejoicing in my sufferings for your sake, and in my flesh I am completing what is lacking in Christ's afflictions for the sake of his body, that is, the church" (Col 1:24).

Paul realizes that the passion and death of the human Jesus of Nazareth was completed and done with on the first Good Friday. Jesus in his finite human body will never suffer and die again. But the universal Body of Christ still on Earth continually suffers and undergoes diminishments, even as it participates in Christ's resurrection. The Cosmic Christ's passion is ongoing, Paul recognizes, and so he consciously redirects the energy required by his physical and emotional afflictions to help this great Body of Christ have the strength to live through its own passion—to its own resurrection (Col 1:24–27). For Paul, everything that happens on Earth is happening in this Universal Christ.

An Evolutionary Perspective on the Passion and Death

It is traditional to see the passion and death of Jesus primarily as his "dying for our sins." In Jesus' day, Hebrew spirituality was focused on sin. While Paul never forgot that Christ died for our sins and that his passion was reparation and redemptive, Paul frequently emphasized a new focus of spirituality, one that centered on God's love and God's grace (Col 3:12–17). In this shift, Paul is taking a forward-looking, cosmic, and evolutionary perspective. In it, God willingly forgives our sins so that we can get back to the important work of transforming the world by our loving service of each other (2 Cor 5:15–17).

Therefore, according to Saint Paul, it is quite legitimate theologically to interpret Jesus' passion and death primarily as a process of rebirth. For Paul, Christ's passion, death, and resurrection are like another baptism for him, a moment of transformation from death to new life. It is a moment of radical change. He is transformed from being merely Jesus of Nazareth into Jesus Christ, the Risen Lord, a New Creation. He is the new Adam in whom we all live and move and have our being (1 Cor 15:45–47). In Paul's view, the passion can also be seen as Jesus going through the pangs of birth. He is giving birth to us and assimilating us as elements of his new Body (2 Cor 5:17). By being baptized into Christ's universal Body, we too are transformed from death into new life (Rom 6:8–11).

The Last Supper: Meditation (Basic Principle 14; Matthew 26:17–35; Mark 14:12–26; Luke 22:7–30; John 13:1—17:26)

In the New Spiritual Exercises, you are asked to focus on the Last Supper as a celebratory dinner with Jesus' closest friends and family. See it as a time for sharing good news and bad.

First Prelude: Even though Jesus is aware of his imminent betrayal and passion, he does not focus on thoughts of suffering. Instead, he treats this Passover meal primarily as a celebration of closeness and a reaffirmation of unity and friendship. In our own lives, the purpose of eating a special meal together is for the nourishment of our bodies and souls. It is also a time for remembering and sharing gifts, especially gifts that can be passed on to new generations. It is, above all, a time for talking about hopes and plans, dreaming and looking into the future. A ritual meal ties together past, present, and future. This is the way Jesus celebrates his last Passover with his friends and family.

Second Prelude: Ask for the graces you need, especially the grace to love the "not-yet."

1. As you read each of the accounts of the Last Supper, notice what Jesus does for his disciples and friends during the Last

Supper. List as many things as you can. For each item on your list, ask Jesus in dialogue why he did this action or shared certain kinds of new knowledge with them. What did he expect them to do with this new knowledge?

2. The key to understanding all the stages of Jesus' passion is his relationship to his Father. What do you learn about this relationship between Jesus and his Father during the Last Supper?

3. Look to see how much of the Last Supper looks to the future, to Jesus' hopes and plans, to what Teilhard calls the "not-yet."

Colloquy: Talk to Christ about your future, your hopes and plans, and what you hope to accomplish for the Body of Christ on Earth.

Agony in the Garden: Meditation (Basic Principle 17; Matthew 26:36–46; Mark 14:32–42; Luke 29:39–46; John 18:1–12)

First Prelude: First, observe Jesus in prayerful dialogue with his Father, then initiate your own dialogue with Jesus.

Second Prelude: Ask for the grace of perseverance in your commitment to Christ. Ask to come into full consciousness of what you have agreed to do for Christ. Ask for the grace of courage. Courage is not the same as fearlessness. Courage is the ability to go forward despite fear, pain, suffering, danger, failure, sin, rejection, and the like.

1. In dialogue with Jesus, ask to identify the consequences of his commitment to his mission and his destiny, to what God wants of his life. Ask also to see the consequences of committing to your destiny, to what God wants of your life. You might find yourself thinking, "This is not what I thought I was getting into." The question to you is: Will you back out or not?

2. What can you learn about the relationship between Jesus and his Father during the agony in the garden? Dialogue with Jesus about this.

3. What can you learn about Jesus' feeling toward his apostles during this event?

Colloquy: Talk to Christ about the fact that you and the rest of us often can't see or predict what might be in the future for us, and ask for the grace to promise to stay the course, to stay committed. Will I agree that I can't be in control of everything that happens, that life isn't made up simply of what I desire? There is a bigger will at work than mine, a grander project to which I am being invited. Will I agree to it? Will I be able to say, "Not my will but yours be done?" My prayer is that I will have the strength and courage to persevere.

Trial before the Sanhedrin: Meditation (Basic Principle 3; Matthew 26; Mark 14; Luke 22; John 18)

Jesus stands up for himself and his purpose, but does not argue or debate with the Jewish authorities. He brings to their consciousness their collective sickness and the contagious spiritual disease they are spreading among the people.

It is not that he doesn't care. In this moment of his life, he has a different focus of energy. He is not about to change the minds of the religious court. This is not the focus of his mission. He doesn't fight the situation. He is not focused on saving his life or escaping his destiny. His task here is to live through his mission with dignity. Nevertheless, even while he is being diminished, he is always trying to bring people to consciousness of what they are doing.

First Prelude: Create in your imagination the scene of Jesus' trial before the Jewish leaders.

Second Prelude: Ask for the graces you will need as you confront those who would keep you from your mission in the Christ Project.

1. In dialogue, ask to become very clear about the true nature of Jesus' mission and the true focus of his energy as it is expressed in this scene.

2. How does Jesus try to bring the religious leaders to consciousness? What does Jesus see as the spiritual disease they are spreading among the people?
3. What are some of the emotional passivities Jesus must endure in this scene?

Colloquy: Renew your commitment to your mission and destiny in Christ and your willingness to endure emotional rejection.

The Trial before Pilate: Meditation (Basic Principle 5; Matthew 27; Mark 15: Luke 23; John 18:28—19:16)

First Prelude: Jesus is clear in his mind, despite the pain and humiliation he is experiencing, that he is operating in the domain of destiny, that is, he is focused on what he must do in order to fulfill his mission for God. He is very clear in saying, "My kingdom is not of this world." His kingdom is not military, not monetary, and not territorial as are most kingdoms of this world.

Second Prelude: His kingdom operates at a different level of existence. Its focus is on the intangible level, the level of values and commitment, the level of quests and destiny, the level of justice, mercy, and love. Ask for the grace to truly identify this intangible and invisible level of existence in your own life and learn to live in it and from within it.

Jesus' Visit to Herod: Meditation (Basic Principle 6; Luke 23:7–12)

First Prelude: Imagine the scene of Jesus in Herod's court.

Second Prelude: Ask for the grace of when to be silent, and how to deal with rejection and mockery when it comes to you.

The Crucifixion: Meditation (Basic Principle 17)

First Prelude: "If you are the Son of God, come down from the cross" (Matt 27:40). The temptation to avoid your destiny is always present. Jesus says, in effect, "No, I won't come down from the cross, even though I could easily do it. I won't come down, because I need to go through this part of my mission to get to the next stage."

Second Prelude: Dying, whether physical or psychological, is always part of a transformation process. Jesus needs to die and be reborn in order to get to the next stage. Ask for the grace to willingly die in spirit, again and again, in order to be reborn into the next stage of your evolution.

TEILHARD'S PRAYER TO THE COSMIC CHRIST:

In the center of your breast I see nothing else than a furnace; and the more I gaze upon this burning hearth, the more it seems to me that, all round about, the contours of your Body are melting, that they are growing great beyond all measure, until I distinguish in you no longer any other features than a world in flames.

—*Hymn to the Universe*

Jesus' Last Words: Meditation (Basic Principle 11)

First Prelude: Jesus' seven final expressions reveal that he continues to carry out his destiny and God-given mission. They also reinforce his awareness of the evolutionary nature of that mission.

Second Prelude: Ask for the grace to see how Jesus, even in these final moments, is always looking toward the future, to the not-yet that remains to be accomplished.

1. "Father, forgive them; for they do not know what they are doing" (Luke 23:34). Forgiveness of sin will remain central throughout the evolutionary process of the Christ Project.

2. "Truly I tell you, today you will be with me in Paradise" (Luke 23:43). Jesus remains focused on the ultimate goal of the Christ Project, to welcome all of creation to be with him forever.

3. "When Jesus saw his mother and the disciple whom he loved standing beside her, he said to his mother, 'Woman, here is your son' " (John 19:26). We are all to be father and mother to everyone with the unconditional love shown by the best parents.

4. "Then he said to the disciple, 'Here is your mother' " (John 19:27). Caring for one another remains the heart of the

Christian mission and the sustaining power of the Universal Christ.

5. "And about three o'clock Jesus cried with a loud voice, 'Eli, Eli, lema sabachthani?' that is, 'My God, my God, why have you forsaken me?' " (Matt 27:46; Mark 15:34). Here Jesus begins to recite Psalm 22. Perhaps he continues quietly reciting the psalm through to the end. You must study this psalm to see what Jesus is truly saying at this point, especially in expressing his deep trust in God despite his suffering. The psalm ends in an evolutionary prayer: "Future generations will be told about the Lord, and proclaim his deliverance to a people yet unborn" (Psalm 22:30–31).

6. "When Jesus knew that all was now finished, he said (in order to fulfill the scripture), 'I am thirsty' " (John 19:28). Jesus, knowing that all was now complete, recalls his prayer to the Father in John 17:4, "I have brought you glory on earth by completing the work you gave me to do." To fulfill that scripture Jesus said, "I thirst." In an evolutionary sense, Jesus expresses here a spiritual thirst that will never end until the Father's program for all of creation is complete (See John 4:13–15; 6:35; 7:37–38).

7. "Then Jesus, crying with a loud voice, said, 'Father, into your hands I commend my spirit' " (Luke 23:46). His final cry as a finite human being is to place his ultimate trust in God. No matter what life throws at us in the future, we commend ourselves to God. We trust that what God has planned for us and for all creation will eventually come about.

End of the Third Week

Journal Review

Before you begin the Fourth Week of the Exercises, it is important to gather and reflect upon the graces and insights of the Third Week. One of the best ways of doing this is to reflectively reread all the entries in your retreat journal, starting from the beginning.

- Set aside at least an hour for this grace-filled process.
- Begin with a prayer for guidance.
- On a fresh page of your journal, write "Third Week Journal Review" and begin listing on this page the insights and graces received.
- As you notice each grace or insight, say a simple thank you to God.
- Close the process with a colloquy of gratitude.

Note: If you are making the Exercises in a small group or team, it may be useful to share with your team members some of what you have written on your Third Week journal review pages.

The Fourth Week

Even though Ignatius names a new "week" in honor of Christ's resurrection and the other glorious mysteries of his risen life, the Third and Fourth Weeks of the Exercises are really the unfolding of one great continuous mystery (Basic Principle 5).

Through his resurrection and his interaction with people thereafter, Jesus remains faithful to his God-given mission on Earth—bringing peace and unity everywhere through compassion, forgiveness, and healing. Although the mission of Jesus of Nazareth, now the risen Lord, has not changed fundamentally, Jesus has been transformed.

During his public life and his passion, the body of Jesus of Nazareth was a finite human body. It needed food, rest, and sleep in order to keep going and could be in only one place at one time. Jesus had to use his two legs to walk if he needed to move from one town to the next. He sweated when the weather was hot.

Now, in his Easter-risen life, the body of Jesus becomes a universal body that incorporates all of us within it. It is no longer a finite, limited body; it is cosmic-sized. It is present everywhere in the universe. It is a divine milieu. You and I no longer simply observe Jesus from the outside, as the disciples did. You and I live in Christ. We experience Christ from inside him, which is where we live (Col 1:18–20). For us, the guarantee of the resurrection generates in us the spiritual energy of joy. Despite our many disappointments and failures, joy and hope are always available when we recognize that we are living, moving, and enjoying life within the great Christ Body (Col 2:6–7).

As for Christ himself, he remains always in relation to his Father. Carrying out the Christ Project is his mission—"until all have become one in him." The guaranteed achievement of the final oneness of all things will reveal the fullness of the mystery of God's love (Col 1:25–27; see also John 6:37–39).

As you make the Exercises, it is important to realize that you—and all of us—are always living in the Fourth Week, because we are always living in the divine milieu, which is the Cosmic Christ Body.

We experience the dynamic of all four Weeks of the Exercises from the perspective of the Fourth Week, that is, we are always praying and reflecting from within the glorious risen Lord (Col 3:12–15).

However, just as the human Jesus of Nazareth had to suffer his passion, so too the evolving Universal Christ in some part of his great body is always undergoing his cosmic passion—when members of his great body suffer pain, hunger, rejection, abuse, torture, misunderstandings, violence, war, murder, and other effects of sin and unavoidable diminishments.

Thus, the continuous single mystery of the passion, death, and resurrection is relived in each person's life and in each human generation by the Universal Christ.

In the call of the Exercises, there is no room for mediocrity. There is only the opportunity for continual improvement in our fidelity and commitment to serve the health and development of the Body of Christ.

The Risen Christ Appears to Mary

Because of Ignatius' special devotion to Mary, he has the risen Lord appear first to her before he appears to anyone else, even though there is no mention of this appearance in scripture (299). Ignatius wants retreatants to be filled with joy, and no one could possibly rejoice more than Mary at her son's resurrection. In this special meeting, let us imagine mother and son discussing God's great evolutionary project, the Christ Project, and the unique contribution to it that she has made and will continue to make (Basic Principle 4).

Mary and the Risen Christ: Meditation (Basic Principle 4)

First Prelude: Imagine Mary early Easter morning praying in the Upper Room that God's will be done for her son. She also remembers her choice to say yes to God many years ago in her garden at the annunciation. And she says yes again.

Second Prelude: In your imagination, join Mary, perhaps, as she steps outside to get a breath of fresh air in the dark, very early morning. See her son appear to her and how they greet one another.

Third Prelude: Ask for the grace to see how the risen Lord can make a great difference in your life and choices. Ask to feel Christ's comforting presence in your life whenever you need it.

1. See Mary and her son talking together, recalling stories from her early life and how they affected her unique contribution to the Christ Project.
2. See Mary as she recalls her Magnificat (Luke 1:46–55) and proudly recites it to her son, who never heard it before. See how he affirms the truth of each line and delights in it as she speaks it.
3. Now imagine the risen Lord showing Mary some of the ways she will influence the Christ Project in the next two thousand years and beyond.

Colloquy: Ask Mary for a deep faith in the risen Lord and for her support in helping you personally in making your unique contribution to the Christ Project.

The Empty Tomb: Meditation (Basic Principle 17)

Prelude: Pray for the Easter grace to acknowledge the empty tomb—that Jesus of Nazareth has truly died. "He is not here." We will no longer be able to cling to that finite Jesus.

Note: We pray to recognize the new, transformed Christ wherever we happen to be. He goes before us. He goes with us. He lives in us and we live in him.

> Christ with me, Christ before me, Christ behind me,
> Christ in me, Christ beneath me, Christ above me,
> Christ on my right, Christ on my left,
> Christ when I lie down, Christ when I sit down,
> Christ when I arise, Christ in the heart of every man who
>   thinks of me,
> Christ in the mouth of every one who speaks of me,
> Christ in the eye of every one who sees me,
> Christ in every ear that hears me.
> —*from Saint Patrick's Breastplate*

You are invited to become conscious of your relationship with this "supreme personal." Without ceasing to recall and love Jesus of Nazareth who walked on the Earth two thousand years ago, you are called in this Fourth Week to learn how to relate in love and gratitude to this supremely personal being who is the Cosmic Christ, in whom you live and move and enjoy your being.

Looking for the New Christ—
the New Creation

In the Scriptures
Disciples on the Road to Emmaus: Meditation—Part I
(Basic Principle 1; Luke 24:13–27, 32)

Prelude: Ask for the grace to read the scriptures in a new way. We no longer look to find only Jesus of Nazareth in the scriptures but to find what the scriptures tell us about our destiny in the Cosmic Christ, to discover hints of the Christ Project of the Father in the religious scriptures and in the revelations that science brings to us. Both of these sources of revelation are our springboard today to discover who we are and who we, as God's creation, are called to be (Luke 24:13–27, 32).

1. Interact with the risen Christ and the disciples as they walk together toward Emmaus. Notice how he shows them a new way to read the scriptures—not to look for him as a human messiah sent to save a small, oppressed nation, but to reveal the new Christ who is source of all life and savior of all creation.

In the Breaking of the Bread
Disciples on the Road to Emmaus: Meditation—Part II
(Basic Principle 17; Luke 24:28–35)

First Prelude: Recall how Christ also reveals himself to the two disciples in the breaking of the bread (Luke 24:28–35). In all the centuries to come, Christians will discover the Cosmic Christ in the breaking of the bread.

Second Prelude: Pray for the grace to discover how you and everyone else are also elements in the eucharistic bread. Pray to live in that consciousness—that we all live and move and have our being in the Christ.

No Limitations in the Risen Christ

Appearance to Disciples in Upper Room: Meditation (Basic Principle 5; Luke 24:36–43 or John 20:19–25)

First Prelude: Recognize the new and unusual abilities of the risen Lord as he comes to his disciples and interacts with them.

Second Prelude: Ask for the grace to realize that "Peace!" is the new Christ greeting to all (John 14:27–31). Ask to know deeply what that greeting requires and implies for those who use it.

1. Explore some of the qualities and abilities of the Cosmic Christ and how you can benefit from them and contribute to them in your work and relationships (John 14:11–14).

From the Way of the Cross to the Way of the Resurrection

Living in the Cosmic Christ: Meditation (Basic Principle 17)

First Prelude: Recall and contrast the diminishments of Jesus during his passion with his dramatic growth in his resurrected and cosmic form.

Second Prelude: Ask for the grace to realize that now in the Cosmic Christ, I am one with Peter, John, Mary of Nazareth, and Mary Magdalene. In Christ, I am also one with Pilate, Herod, the high priests, the Pharisees, and all the others. They are all still alive in the great Christ.

1. We bring Jesus of Nazareth with us in the great Christ, and we bring his passion and death with us, since all these events live forever in the Cosmic Christ.
2. As Henry Nouwen once said, "Hope is not about the fulfillment of desires. It is not about belief in the impossible. Instead, hope enables people to sustain life's defeats and disappointments in the faith of Jesus Christ."

Thomas Who Doubts: Meditation (Basic Principle 15; John 20:26–29)

First Prelude: Picture the scene between Jesus and Thomas.
Second Prelude: Ask for the grace to realize the depth and universality of forgiveness available to us, to realize how precious is the gift of faith, and to feel deep gratitude for it.

1. Recognize that the apostles do not reject Thomas because he refuses to believe in the resurrection. Share your own doubts and fears.
2. Recognize how Saint Paul responded to the gifts of forgiveness and faith and how he prays for it for others (Col 1:11–14).

Being Sent—Individually and Collectively

Peter's Assignment at the Sea of Galilee: Meditation (Basic Principle 9; John 21:15–17)

First Prelude: To see Peter as himself and as a symbol of all the disciples, then and now. To hear the risen Lord's triple request: "Feed my lambs.…Tend my sheep.…Feed my sheep" (John 21:15–17).

Second Prelude: Pray for the grace to understand deeply what the words: "Feed my lambs.…Tend my sheep.…Feed my sheep" may mean for me in my work and my relationships.

The Ascension: Meditation—Part I (Basic Principle 10; Matthew 28:18–20)

First Prelude: The disciples are being sent individually and as a group to go all over Earth and spread the good news.

Second Prelude: Ask for the grace to make (or renew) the generous gift of yourself to the ongoing work of the Cosmic Christ. Review the offering you made to Christ and the Father in the meditation on the Call of Christ.

1. Dialogue with Christ who is about to return to the Father and who is now blessing you and sending you forth.

The Ascension: Meditation—Part II (Basic Principle 17; Mark 16:15, 19–20)

First Prelude: For Teilhard, the ascension was the most beautiful feast of the year, since it is a foreshadowing of the final consummation of the universe returning to the Father, the grand fulfillment that we all anticipate as we live in Christ. Nevertheless, since in his ascension we are all already living in his great Body, in him we too have already ascended to the Father. Insofar as we are in him as part of his Cosmic Body, we are already in heaven enjoying the communion of all the saints (Col 3:1–4).

Second Prelude: The grace we seek at the ascension is twofold.

First, no longer are we to focus all our attention on Jesus of Nazareth. Instead, we also focus on the work that Teilhard calls the "not-yet" Body of Christ, the divine body of which we are a part, the universal body that is still growing and maturing. Saint Paul learned that the focus of spiritual growth and maturity happens now for us, not only by focusing on the finite Jesus but also by *committing ourselves to the Christ Project, to the evolving Cosmic Christ, the Christ in whom we live.* Saint Paul says he is committed to the "Christ in you, the hope of glory. It is he whom we proclaim, training everyone and teaching everyone in all wisdom, so that we may present everyone mature in Christ. For this I toil and struggle with all the energy that he powerfully inspires within me" (Col 1:27–29).

Second, because the tomb is empty and because Jesus has departed from Earth in his finite physical body, we ask for the grace *to see Christ as he is with us today—the Christ in each other and in creation.* Individually and collectively, we are to seek and care for the Christ who lives in our brothers and sisters and in our planet. Like Paul, we work to train and teach each other so that everyone may grow mature in Christ.

Infused with the Divine Spirit

Pentecost and the Life Energy of the Divine Milieu: Meditation (Basic Principle 2; Acts 2:1–4)

First Prelude: Making the entire world conscious of the great Christ Project became the task of the apostles—and it is ours. To be baptized is to formally and consciously become a member of the Body of Christ. Nevertheless, the mission is to invite all men and women, whatever their religious beliefs, to live the way of peace and justice. This is the broader work, the collective work: to spread peace and justice, to show compassion and forgiveness to all, to build a better world for everyone, especially the poor, the sick, the deprived, the forgotten, the lonely, etc.

Second Prelude: Pray for the grace to welcome the Holy Spirit and the strength and courage to carry out your commitment to the Cosmic Christ and the Christ Project.

1. On Pentecost, the church sings its evolutionary hymn, reminding us that there is much work yet to be done in the Christ Project, which is why we need the Holy Spirit's fire.

Come, Holy Spirit, fill the hearts of your faithful.
Enkindle in us the fire of your love,
And we shall be recreated,
And you shall renew the face of the Earth.

Recreating humanity and renewing the face of the Earth describes not only the evolutionary and continuous work assigned to the Holy Spirit, but it is also a summary description of the Christ Project.

The Final Contemplation: Relating to the Father from within the Cosmic Christ

The Way God Loves

You began the New Spiritual Exercises with the *Contemplatio ad Amorem*, where you learned how *to love the way God loves.* You now finish the New Spiritual Exercises with the same *Contemplatio ad Amorem.*

Recall the two important spiritual truths that go with this contemplation:

> The first emphasizes that love ought to manifest itself more by deeds than by words.
> The second says that love entails a reciprocal sharing between lover and beloved.

The grace we want is to be able to respond appropriately to this divine Lover, to love the way that divine Lover loves.

Four Developmental Stages

Recall the four ways or developmental stages by which God expresses love. First, God gives gifts. Second, God remains present with the gifts and alongside the recipient, you. Third, God keeps acting (and laboring) in and through those gifts, as well as in and through you. Fourth, God shares the divine Self (the ultimate gift) with you.

Be with God as God practices these four ways of showing love to you—and to all of creation—and then ask God what God has in mind for you to do—how you can reciprocate loving God and all of creation in a similar fourfold manner.

The human family and all of creation are, in fact, alive in the living Body of the Cosmic Christ. To love the body is to love its head, for the two are one being. Teilhard would not have us avoid the world or try to withdraw from it, but to plunge into it, for Christ's sake, with open and loving hearts and minds. To forget this "finding

God in all things" perspective is to miss the grandeur and greatness of God's salvific plan for creation.

Learning to Love the Way God Loves: The Contemplation

First Prelude: Using your imagination, picture God wishing to express the God head outside Itself, as it were, by creating a universe that would reflect God's creative love, a universe that God could watch and delight in—from outside and from within—as it grew and developed over many billions of years through the evolutionary Law of Attraction-Connection-Complexity-Consciousness. Finally, picture how the human race emerges from the evolving Earth, a people who can be conscious of how much God loves them.

Second Prelude: You may picture the Trinity looking, as it were, at the human race and wanting to be lovingly involved with them, giving gifts to people individually and collectively.

Third Prelude: You may ask for the grace to respond generously to such love by learning to love the way God loves, that is, to love God and those around you in the same fourfold way.

1. THE FIRST STAGE OF LOVING: GIVING GIFTS

At the first stage of the *Contemplatio*, Ignatius tells us, God gives gifts. Love is shown in action. Giving gifts is an action. It is more than words. All of creation is God's gift to us. Creation is the Original Blessing.

For example, in this and the following points, consider the vastness of the universe with its galaxies, stars, planets—many hundreds of billions of them—and its almost fourteen billion years of evolving existence. Consider the inert elements of Earth, the metals, minerals, and gases. Consider the organic elements. Consider microscopic life—microbes evolving through bacteria, viruses, and molds, then, over eons of time, to insects, fish, reptiles, plants, grasses, trees, and animals. Consider consciousness becoming an emergent property of life, and how humans, over the past thirty thousand years, also created language, art and music, forms of government, science, literature, and all the other elements of civilization and culture. Still, the evolutionary process keeps moving ahead.

On the microscopic side, science has revealed the incredible complexity and activity of each living being—the human genome, the trillions of cells that live in our bodies, each with its own highly complex intra-active life.

Recognize the evolutionary Law of Attraction-Connection-Complexity-Consciousness that God has placed in every particle God created, and that this law is designed to culminate in the spiritualization of all matter. Through our faith, we have come to believe that all creation lives in, with, and through God in a divine milieu, so that in this divine milieu we all live and move and have our being, and that there is nothing outside this divine milieu (see, for example, Paul's speech in Acts 17:22–31).

Recognize the gift of Earth itself, our home planet. All the beauties of mountains, plains, and skies. All the power of tornadoes, hurricanes, tidal waves, floods, deserts, and frozen tundra.

Add to this all the gifts you have personally received—talents, skills, education, opportunities, family, friends. Don't forget your five senses, as well as your memory, intelligence, willpower, imagination, freedom to choose, the ability to love and make commitments, the ability to accomplish things, to build teams, to worship, etc.

After you have contemplated and reflected upon all of God's gifts, you are invited to reply to the Divine Giver in a colloquy.

Colloquy: Perhaps you can offer your *gifts* to God, to show that you have grasped this first level of love. For Ignatius, your liberty, memory, understanding, and will are the best of what any human possesses. Ignatius suggests you express yourself to God in the following, or a similar, way:

> Take, Lord, and receive all my liberty, my memory, my understanding, and my entire will—all that I have and possess. You have given them to me; I return them to you, Lord. Everything is yours. Dispose of it all according to your will. Give me the grace to love you, and that is enough for me (234).

2. THE SECOND STAGE OF LOVING: PRESENCE

At the second stage, where the lover is present to the gifts, Ignatius suggests you contemplate each of the areas of creation mentioned in the First Point and observe how God does not depart from us after giving these gifts but remains lovingly present to each of them. Conclude with a colloquy.

Although, traditionally, directors suggest that the "Take and Receive" prayer may be repeated after each of the four stages, Ignatius allows the retreatant to proceed "in the manner described in the first point, or in any other way you feel to be better."[1] Perhaps, such a second-stage prayer, emphasizing mutual presence, might go something like this:

> Just as you, God, remain present with your gifts and just as you remain present to me, I choose to remain actively present to the gifts I offer to you, God, by not wasting them or disregarding them or never using them, but rejoicing in using them for your purposes and for your greater glory. In my loving of you, I wish also to remain present to you. To do this, I beg the grace to remain conscious that I am always in your presence and with Christ helping to build the Great Christ Body.

3. THE THIRD STAGE OF LOVING: COOPERATIVE INTERACTION

The third stage of loving focuses on *personal and active interaction.* In Ignatius' words, "I will consider how God labors and works for me in all the creatures on the face of the earth" (236).

God doesn't just act once, and then stop. God continues acting and interacting at every moment with, in, and through the gifts God

---

1. In the *Thesaurus Spiritualis Societatis Jesu* (Rome: Jesuit Curia, 1953), Father Roothaan, SJ, in his footnotes on this point of the *Contemplatio,* focusing on the word *better,* suggests that the retreatant might formulate a response different from the "Take and Receive" prayer of the First Point, a response that might not only be better but also would recognize the advance—the *magis*—reflected in this point's theme of *presence.* In later notes, Father Roothaan makes similar suggestions, that each colloquy reflect the *magis*—the advanced expression of love—in each subsequent point.

gives in creation. So, for us to love in the same interactive way, we need to continue acting and interacting with the gifts we already possess and the gifts continually being given to us, so as to help creation to grow and evolve in complexity and consciousness.

This third stage of loving again invites a new level of a prayer, one of interactive commitment beyond the original "Take and Receive" prayer. It might take a form something like:

> Ever-working God, in reflecting on your almost fourteen billion years of divine revelation and original blessing, I have come to recognize the Law of Attraction-Connection-Complexity-Consciousness that you have placed in me and in every particle of matter you created, and that this law is designed to culminate in the spiritual transformation of all matter. Therefore, I dedicate myself, for your greater glory, to growing in complexity and consciousness by working alongside others—in Christ—with those talents and gifts you have given me. I will strive to find ever-new ways to bring to their highest expression and capacity the material things in my life.

4. THE FOURTH STAGE OF LOVING: MUTUAL INDWELLING

In the fourth stage, God shares the divine Self (the ultimate gift) with you and me, including divine qualities of justice, goodness, piety, mercy, and so forth. God does not only give gifts that are external to the Godself, as it were, but gives that Godself to us as an active, involved, interactive personal presence—just as the sun's rays give us the sun itself in an active and interactive presence.

The physical incarnation of the Divine Word in becoming a human being is one way God shared the divine Self and demonstrates this fourth stage of loving. Christ's mystical incarnation in the Eucharist is another primary symbol of this self-giving of God to us. In the Universal Christ, we are offered a way to reciprocate this self-giving kind of love, so that with Saint Paul, we can say, "I no longer live, but I am alive in Christ" (Gal 2:20).

At the fourth stage of showing love, Ignatius wants us to learn to live our day and our destiny within God the Beloved. We live out our day within and alongside our Beloved, that is, we remain present in the gifts we offer to God, acting in and through those gifts as well as in and through the Beloved.

After all, at every moment God is keeping everything in being, from the smallest microbe to the farthest galaxy. God and we are acting and working side-by-side (Stage Three) and as one (Stage Four). We are working on the Christ Project together—God in me and I in God. In this way, each of us, individually and together, learns to become a "contemplative in action."

To express in prayer this fourth way of loving in a colloquy, we might say something like:

O Great God, I no longer wish simply to work for you. My deepest desire and the grace I ask is that I may live consciously in you and with you and as a part of your Christ, that I may realize that my primary privilege and honor is to be a cell in the Cosmic Body of Christ. I wish to live and work no longer just as me, but consciously as part of Christ—on our way to you. I desire to know and see how the Christ Body as a whole is working toward its fulfillment, and I wish to cooperate consciously and ever more generously with whatever you wish and desire.

CONCLUSION

It is essential not to rush through this contemplation. It is the summation and high point of the Exercises and of all the graces you can expect from the Exercises. The richness and graces that flow from this contemplation are inexhaustible.

It is also important to remember that, while this contemplation engenders in you a deeply personal relationship with the Creator, its primary purpose is to help you discover your God-given destiny and to develop you as a four-level lover of others, of nature, and of all creation.

End of the Fourth Week

Journal Review

Take some time to gather and reflect upon the graces and insights of the Fourth Week. Reflectively reread all the entries in your retreat journal, starting from the beginning.

- Begin with a prayer for guidance.
- On a fresh page of your journal, write "Fourth Week Journal Review" and begin listing on this page the insights and graces received.
- As you notice each grace or insight, say a simple thank you to God.
- Review any discernment or decisions you have made.
- Close the process with a colloquy of gratitude.

Note: If you are making the Exercises in a small group or team, it may be useful to share with your team members some of what you have written on your Fourth Week journal review pages.

Appendix A: Steps in a Group Contemplation

- Each participant reads over the instructional material for the contemplation ahead of time.
- During the prayer, participants sit on chairs in a tight circle, knees almost touching.
- It is useful in group contemplation to appoint a starter person.
- Let the starter person remind everyone that you are in the presence of God, that God surrounds and penetrates each of you and the group as a whole.
- The starter may offer aloud a prayer for the grace appropriate to this contemplation.
- The starter person may invite others, in turn, to add to this prayer.
- The group may then begin reading aloud the assigned scripture passage, perhaps taking turns, beginning with the starter and moving to the right, so that each person reads a sentence or two of the passage. In some cases, it may be beneficial for the group to read the scripture passage twice.
- When the scripture reading is done, after a few moments of silence, the starter person describes—for no more than 20 or 30 seconds—what is happening in his or her personal contemplative experience, that is, what is happening in his or her imagination, thoughts, or feelings. Then the starter passes the turn to the person on the right. This may easily be done by touching the knee of the person on the right.
- In general, each person's turn to speak lasts usually about 20 or 30 seconds but not more than a minute.

Each person shares aloud what is happening in his or her imagination or thoughts.

- When sharing, use a soft voice, but with enough volume so that the others in the small group can hear you without effort.
- People often find it easier to contemplate a scene if they close their eyes during the process.
- When each person has finished sharing during the first round, he or she should gently tap the knee of the person to the right, indicating that it is now that person's turn to share for the next 20 or 30 seconds.
- The process continues, circling repeatedly around the group until the contemplation time is over.
- If, by chance, you have nothing to say when your turn comes, or you wish to give up your turn, you can either remain silent for a few seconds before you pass it on, or you may simply immediately pass the turn to the person on your right.
- Be courteous not to monopolize the sharing by going on and on without pause. If you have much more to share, save it until your turn comes around again.
- Do not worry if others, when they speak, seem to be in a scene different from the scene that you see. Your imagination is quite capable of holding three or four different images or contexts simultaneously.
- When the prayer time is almost over, the starter may suggest the group begin their colloquies, i.e., speaking directly to God, Jesus, the Holy Spirit, or Mary. Using the same turn-by-turn process, people can make their colloquies aloud or in silence. It builds people's faith if you speak your prayer aloud.
- You may cycle around the group more than once if persons wish to make additional colloquies.
- After it feels as though everyone has finished with the contemplation, the starter may suggest that people open their eyes and begin a spontaneous shared reflection. Here the sharing does not have to follow any particular order or turns.

- Be sure to thank your prayer partners for the time spent together.
- Later, in private, record your reflections in your personal journal. You may also make note of any insights you have received from others.

Appendix B: How to Choose Music for Prayer

Ignatius loved music but unfortunately didn't have it readily available as we do today, in many recorded forms. With electronic systems, we have access to a wide variety of music for listening in public, in private, or as background. Well-chosen music may be used to foster the mood of a specific prayer exercise or the spirit of the day.

Some General Rules

If you choose to listen to music during a meditation or contemplation, normally:

- *It should nurture and reinforce the mood of the exercise.* Thus, in general, somber music is appropriate during considerations of sin; quietly reflective music during the First Week; energetic and forward moving music during the Second Week; sad and sorrowful music during the Third Week; and joyful music during the Fourth Week.
- For the most part, *it should be music without lyrics* so as not to distract or intrude on the prayer experience, except when the lyrics are truly helpful and deepen the prayer. Lyrics in Latin or a language foreign to the retreatant are acceptable, such as Gregorian chant or a Requiem Mass.
- *It should NOT be music that might generate personal distracting or disturbing associations with your past or present life.* Such music may hinder your ability to remain present to the prayer experience.

Appropriate Choices for Prayer Experiences

Since music-listening tastes differ widely and new music keeps appearing daily, it makes no sense to offer a bibliography of music recordings here. Rather, depending on your taste, your preference should be to use music that supports your mood or emotion appropriate to the prayer experience.

Music During the Day

For listening between formal prayer times, various kinds of religious music are preferred. These include classical religious music of Bach, Beethoven, Fauré, and many others; forms of church music, gospel music, hymns, psalms and chants; and so-called spirit or spiritual music often broadcast on religious stations, which may be performed in the style of folk music, rock, or blues. Any or all of these can be helpful, when well chosen, to foster and maintain a prayerful spirit.

Consult Your Guide

If you are using music either to deepen your contemplative state in prayer or to maintain a certain spiritual mood between prayer times, please report this to your guide or director. Also, tell your guide how well or how poorly music is working for you. Not all people are helped in prayer by music. If music is not proving helpful to your prayer or distracting you for the retreat's purpose, your guide may suggest you change the kinds of music you are listening to, or may suggest you spend a few days in silence without music.

Appendix C: Dialogue Prayer

The reason for introducing a dialogue prayer form during a contemplative prayer exercise is to enable the retreatant to interact verbally with a figure, for example, Jesus or Mary, in order to access more clearly the wisdom of the figure and to build a relationship with the figure. Dialogue differs from contemplation in that the verbal exchange of the dialogue is the primary focus of the exercise, so much so that the words experienced in the dialogue are meant to be captured on paper in the midst of the exercise.

In the repetition of a meditation or contemplation, the dialogue format may be used, usually to get more deeply or accurately into the meaning and purpose of the exercise for your life.

Steps in Dialogue Prayer

1. During preparation for a spiritual exercise and before a formal dialogue prayer begins, it is helpful to prepare a few opening questions that you would like to ask the figure(s) during the prayer. Depending on the result you hope for from the dialogue, your questions may be very specific or remain rather general. For example, some generic questions you might ask the figure are:

    *   What did you think, feel, or do during this event?
    *   What is the meaning of this event for me?
    *   What do you want me to learn from you?

2. Once you are into the contemplative prayer experience and the figure has come alive in your imagination, picture yourself present to the figure, or in some way sense the presence of the figure, so that the two of you are together. Using whatever imaginal senses work best for you—seeing, hear-

ing, touching, smelling, tasting—picture the scene in enough detail to see or feel yourselves together clearly.

3. Open the dialogue by writing down your first question and picture yourself asking it of the figure.

4. Next, write down whatever response seems to come from the figure. At first, responses from the figure may seem forced, artificial, or difficult. Don't let this stop you. Those feelings will change and, after a few exchanges, the dialogue will feel much more natural and spontaneous. As you write, don't worry about grammar or spelling; just allow the process to flow.

5. Let the dialogue take its own course. You may not even need to use the rest of the questions you prepared.

6. Continue writing out the dialogue, asking questions or responding to questions the figure may ask you, until you run out of questions and the dialogue feels complete or at least has reached a stopping place.

7. You may always ask a final question or two, for example:

- Is there anything else I should know or think about?
- Is there any other figure I should dialogue with?
- Do you have a gift for me?
- Is there something you want from me?

8. After the colloquy and during your review, it is always helpful to reread your dialogue and perhaps to underline some important phrases or images.

Note: When writing a dialogue in your journal, it is helpful to record it as if it were a dramatic script, beginning each new question or comment with a letter (such as the first letter of your name, L for Louis) that indicates it is you talking and the first letter of the figure's name (such as J for Jesus and M for Mary) when the figure is responding. So, a page in your journal might look like:

L: How did you feel when you were baptized and heard God speak to you?

J: It came as a total surprise. I hadn't felt God's presence like that in a long time. When was there a time you felt God's presence so strongly?

L: I think I was in high school before I graduated. It was at a retreat.

J: I was a little older when I felt my Father's presence. Just before I left Nazareth to come here. It was as if I was being pushed from inside to come here.

L: At your baptism, what did John the Baptist say when he heard God's voice? Did he tell you?

J: He was surprised and delighted. I think he even laughed. He said to me, "It's you, then, cousin. You're the one I have been announcing all along."

L: etc.

Appendix D: Meditation— Eastern and Western

Since many people today have heard about or even practiced Eastern forms of meditation, it seems a good idea to clarify what Christians traditionally mean by the term meditation.

The Christian and the Buddhist both want to reach God, but their understanding of meditation comes from different spiritual traditions. Buddha came from a tradition where meditation meant sitting quietly for periods striving for a silent and motionless mind to enter pure consciousness. In contrast, Jesus emphasized prayer that used words, images, metaphors, faith, and knowledge, all of which required activity of the mind and will.

Many people, Easterners and Westerners, including Christians, have found deep relaxation and inner peace when practicing Buddhist meditation. Indeed, such spiritual exercises could be and have been adapted as mentally quiet forms of Christian prayer. Hints of this type of prayer may be found in some psalms. "Be still and know that I am God" (Psalm 46) and "Be still before the Lord and wait patiently for him" (Psalm 37).

In an Appendix in the original Spiritual Exercises on various methods of prayer, Ignatius suggests a method that has an Eastern resonance and is similar to the "Jesus Prayer," which using various formulas (what the Buddhists would call *mantras*) was practiced and taught by the Greek Fathers and has continued in popularity to our own day, promoted especially by Trappist monks.

Christian Meditation

Nevertheless, the meaning of meditation in the Spiritual Exercises and in much of Christian tradition focuses on exercising your mental and reflective powers, specifically your memory, intellect, and will.

The Latin root for the word *meditation* is the same root as the verb used to describe the action of a cow chewing its cud. Cows—sheep, too—after eating the green grasses regurgitate certain substances in their stomachs and chew them over again in order to get more nutrition from them. The good shepherd knows his sheep need green grass. "The Lord is my shepherd, I shall not want. He makes me lie down in green pastures" (Psalm 23:1–2). The divine shepherd knows that we need "green pastures" filled with spiritual food, and we need time to fully digest this food. In a similar way, during a meditation you are invited to focus on a familiar spiritually powerful event, image, or saying, e.g., from the life of Christ, and mentally chew on it over and over, each time getting more insight or spiritual nutrition from it.

In fact, when you receive a new insight or get additional clarity meditating on a certain spiritual event, Ignatius would ask you to stay with it, rest in it, and come back to it at a later prayer period in what he calls a "repetition."

Christian meditation is not designed to produce deep relaxation or even, as a rule, inner peace. Some meditative insights may prove disturbing or upsetting. For example, in prayer, you may discover you need to change your way of looking at poor people, realize the wounding of personal sin, leave a relationship, or even begin a new, unfamiliar career. The Spiritual Exercises as a whole are focused primarily on helping you make decisions and discover your God-given destiny. Either process could prove unsettling.

Desires

In general, Eastern meditation, especially Buddhism, uses meditation to help you get beyond "desires," since Buddha taught that having desires was a major source of suffering. In contrast, in the Christian tradition, you are expected to have desires, for yourself and for the kingdom of God. Jesus speaks of having desires. Much of his discourse at the Last Supper as recorded in John's Gospel is about his desires for the future of his young community of followers. Saint Paul encourages us to desire with all our strength to serve the growth and development of the Body of Christ. Suffering is often a natural consequence even of holy desires. In this sense, Buddha was correct, desires bring suffering. However, for Christians, such suffering is to be willingly endured for the sake of promoting God's evolutionary plan for creation.

Contemplation

While meditation in the Spiritual Exercises uses mainly the mental powers of memory, intellect, and will, contemplation uses the human faculty of imagination with all its sensory and emotional capacities. As you know, on a cold winter day you may daydream about basking in the sun on a summer beach. You can do this because the imagination possesses its own complete set of sensory powers— its own inner eyes, ears, nose, taste, and touch. When the imagination's senses are active and focused on creating a scene, they can generate corresponding feelings and emotions.

In most Eastern forms of meditation, with a few exceptions, the conscious use of the imagination is not encouraged. When images or ideas spontaneously arise during meditation, the meditator is told to simply let them pass by, and pay no more attention to them than one would to a twig floating by in a stream. In contrast, in Christian prayer, using the imagination is strongly encouraged, since it is a most powerful and integrative faculty—and very useful in an evolutionary spirituality, since it can envision the "not-yet."

Your imagination is the only faculty that can integrate your body, mind, and spirit as well as the past, present, and future. Through your imagination, you can bring the past into the present and allow it to live again. For example, during Christian contemplation, you are asked to use your imagination to create a scene—the nativity, Jesus healing the blind man, Jesus on the cross, etc.—and to enter it as deeply as you can. Perhaps at the nativity, using your imagination, you might picture yourself as a shepherd or one of the workers at the inn. At a healing, you might picture yourself as one of Jesus' disciples or as the person being healed. At the crucifixion, you might place yourself near Mary or among the Roman soldiers there.

The point in contemplation is that, instead of merely pondering or thinking about an event in Jesus' life, you become a participant in it and, in this way, you see, hear, and feel what it is like to be near Jesus. You enter into his mind and spirit. Once you are "in" the contemplation, the process becomes spontaneous because you are there, involved. You may strike up a conversation with Mary, or Jesus may ask you to do something.

When you contemplate a sacred event deeply enough, it produces its effects on you. You may begin to see more clearly who you were meant to be, how you may need to change your view of the world, and how you are called to enter the mind and heart of Jesus. Some have suggested that Jesus frequently used contemplative prayer. For example, through contemplation, Jesus himself may have become aware, long before the passion events unfolded, of the suffering he would have to endure.

Some saints have said that when you get deeply involved in contemplation over a long period, you are led to a kind of mental silence or quiet, where both the intellect and the imagination grow totally still. At this point, you enter a deeper reality. The feeling of being totally accepted by God arises. You feel the loving embrace of God.

Contemplation is a fascinating process since it begins as a very conscious and focused kind of daydreaming that can lead you to God and to God-consciousness. As you go through the Spiritual Exercises, you will see why so many holy men and women have used this contemplative method of prayer to enliven, deepen, and clarify their spiritual journey. They also remind us not to expect results too quickly.

Intellectual Visions in Contemplation

In the normal process of Ignatius' contemplative prayer, persons usually experience imaginative visions, where the imagination's "picturing faculty" would help them vividly experience a scene from Jesus' life. In contrast, Ignatius was primarily an intellectual mystic. The personal contemplations of Ignatius produced predominantly "intellectual visions or insights." These moments of conceptual clarity might help Ignatius better understand spiritual truths or earlier insights; or they might be new ideas; or they might modify or coordinate a series of ideas never before connected.[1]

---

1. George E. Ganss, SJ, ed. *Ignatius of Loyola: Spiritual Exercises and Selected Works*, a volume in the Paulist Classics of Western Spirituality series (New York: Paulist Press, 1991), 30.

Teilhard, too, may have been an intellectual mystic rather than a "picturing" one, where in his prayer he was able to tie together and integrate a number of scientific facts with theological ones. This preference of Ignatius and Teilhard should provide some consolation for those who do not find it natural to "picture" biblical scenes. One of Ignatius' most profound contemplative experiences was an auditory one, hearing sounds that brought theological understanding. (See Optional Activity below.)

OPTIONAL ACTIVITY: THE MUSICAL CHORD

Ignatius, standing on the banks of the River Cardoner, had a mystical musical experience that allowed him to understand the Holy Trinity. You can get a taste of his experience if you have access to a piano keyboard.

First, depress the key called middle C, and listen to its solitary sound; this is the sound of the Creator. Let go of the C note and now press the E key, two keys above the C, and listen to its solitary sound; it is the sound of the Redeemer. Let go of the E note and press the G key, two keys above the E, and listen to its solitary sound; this is the sound of the Holy Spirit, the Sanctifier.

Now, press all three keys, C, E, and G, simultaneously and listen to the sound of the musical chord. It is the sound of the Trinity. It is a more complex sound than the sound of any individual note. While its sound is different from any of the distinct single note sounds, it contains all of them. The Holy Trinity always acts as a chord. The three persons are always in consonance.

green press
INITIATIVE

Paulist Press is committed to preserving ancient forests and natural resources. We elected to print this title on 30% post consumer recycled paper, processed chlorine free. As a result, for this printing, we have saved:

5 Trees (40' tall and 6-8" diameter)
2 Million BTUs of Total Energy
500 Pounds of Greenhouse Gases
2,410 Gallons of Wastewater
146 Pounds of Solid Waste

Paulist Press made this paper choice because our printer, Thomson-Shore, Inc., is a member of Green Press Initiative, a nonprofit program dedicated to supporting authors, publishers, and suppliers in their efforts to reduce their use of fiber obtained from endangered forests.

For more information, visit www.greenpressinitiative.org

Environmental impact estimates were made using the Environmental Defense Paper Calculator. For more information visit: www.papercalculator.org.